MASTERING IMMIGRATION & NATURALIZATION RECORDS

3rd Edition
Volume II of Quillen's Essentials of Genealogy

www.essentialgenealogy.com

"Your book *Secrets of Tracing your Ancestors* has been extremely helpful to me in a renewal of my genealogy interests." – Nancy Dailey

"I would like to thank you for writing a very informative book. There was a lot of information that I did not know about…" – Donna Perryman Moon

"I purchased your book and have found it most helpful." – Glenda Laney

"Thanks for your help and for writing your excellent book!" – Laura Johnson

"I have enjoyed reading your book and I've found excellent leads for finding ancestors." – Donna Mann

"… It is not only informative but entertaining. Incorporating your own experiences in brought the book to life. Again, thank you for helping me to understand the many aspects of genealogy and for supplying a roadmap to finding more information about our ancestors." – Dana L. Hager

"Of all the books I have looked at yours is the best…and you write with your heart and soul. Thanks for writing such a great book." – Karen Dredge

"I got this book out of the library, but before I was half-way through it, I decided I had to have my own copy. Lots of helpful suggestions! I'd recommend it for all new and experienced family historians." – Margaret Combs

"I am embarking on the family history journey and have found your book to be very helpful … thanks for putting together a helpful, easy to follow guide." – Suzanne Adams

"I'm absolutely delighted that I discovered your book "Secrets of Tracing Your Ancestors." I've only been at this for a month (to keep sane during knee surgery recuperation) and now I'm hooked." – Cecily Bishop

About the Author

For more than 20 years, W. Daniel Quillen has been a professional writer specializing in travel and technical subjects. He has taught beginning genealogy courses to university students and working adults, is a frequent lecturer in beginning and intermediate genealogy classes, and speaks at regional genealogy conferences. He has compiled his years of genealogical training and research into a growing series of genealogy how-to books. He lives in Centennial, Colorado with his wife and children. If you would like to contact Dan about anything in this book, his e-mail address is: wdanielquillen@gmail.com.

MASTERING IMMIGRATION & NATURALIZATION RECORDS

3rd Edition
Volume II of Quillen's Essentials of Genealogy

www.essentialgenealogy.com

W. Daniel Quillen

Author of *Secrets of Tracing Your Ancestors*; *The Troubleshooter's Guide to Do-It-Yourself Genealogy*; and *Quillen's Essentials of Genealogy* books, a new series of genealogy primers

Cold Spring Press

COLD SPRING PRESS
www.essentialgenealogy.com

3rd Edition

PHOTO CREDITS

Cover design by Matthew Simmons (www.myselfincluded.com). The following photos are from flickr.com: front cover by Gilles Dubois; back cover by Per Ola Wiberg ~ Powi; page 71; Kheel Center via flickr.com; page 132 by HA! Designs-ArtbyHeather; p. 141: sakraft1; p. 142: staypuftman; p. 143: crabchick.

To contact the author directly, e-mail him at: wdanielquillen@gmail.com. And please check out Dan's blog at www.essentialgenealogy.com/blog.

TABLE OF CONTENTS

MASTERING
IMMIGRATION &
NATURALIZATION
RECORDS

1. INTRODUCTION

Welcome to the world of searching for your immigrant ancestors! If you have made any efforts at all, you have probably been amazed at the number and quality of immigration and naturalization records available to genealogists. These records assist your search for your immigrant ancestors. Sometimes those records are difficult, expensive or time-consuming to find. But – keep your head up and in the game. New collections of immigration and naturalization records are coming online all the time, making your search easier.

This book has been organized to help you search out those of your ancestors who came to the United States from distant lands – whether Europe, South America, or from our neighbors to the north and south: Canada and Mexico.

Many of the records available to researchers whose ancestors came from outside the United States have been overlooked for years. But researchers are beginning to become aware of the value of these records. In addition, there are organizations that have been working hard to get permission to convert all those wonderful records to digital format so that they can be put on the Internet. Once there, anyone can access them and glean tremendous amounts of genealogical information from them. Thanks and a tip o' the hat to subscription organizations like Ancestry.com, Fold3.com and others, as well as organizations that provide information for free: the LDS Church through FamilySearch.org, for example. Organizations like these work tirelessly to digitize records that have for years (centuries) been only found in dusty courthouses and other out-of-the-way places.

Thanks to all those who are working to digitize immigration and naturalization records!

Much of my own family research has focused on US collections. Most of my family lines came to America during its earliest years: a Mayflower passenger, one who braved the wilds of America in the 1630s, and others who came here early in our nation's history. In fact, a number of my ancestors fought to establish the United States as a free and independent nation.

Because of that, I have only in recent years expanded my searches to the immigration and naturalization records available. What genealogical treasures these records are! Questions asked and answered provide incredible information and insight into my ancestors, their lives and their family members' lives.

As I have done with other genealogy books I have written (*Secrets of Tracing Your Ancestors, The Troubleshooter's Guide to Do-It-Yourself Genealogy*, and the six titles in *Quillen's Essentials of Genealogy* series), I will use some of my ancestors to demonstrate research tactics. Because many of my direct-line ancestors came to the US hundreds of years ago, I will use distant cousins who came more recently to demonstrate some of the options available to you for searching immigration and naturalization records. For example, Teague McQuillan, the first of my ancestors to come to America, stepped on our shores about 250 years before Ellis Island opened her doors for business, and her arms to embrace those who were immigrating to America. It wouldn't do much good to search Ellis Island's passenger lists for him, as good as they may be!

But, many McQuillans followed their ancestor Teague to the US, and many of them entered America through Ellis Island, as well as many other ports of entry. So I'll use some of those later cousins – Cunningham, Sellers, McQuillan, Peoples, Stunkard, McCollough and others, as we introduce various immigration and naturalization records of interest to genealogists.

Earlier in this section I mentioned several other genealogy books I have written. Let me expand a bit, as one or more of them may be of interest and help to you as you head down the genealogical turnpike:

If you are just beginning, consider picking up *Secrets of Tracing Your Ancestors*. This book is targeted at those just beginning their genealogical journey, and will start you at the very beginning, with organization and where to find information close at hand. It then provides you with techniques and strategies for finding your ancestors. Reviewers have even observed that there are tactics and information in the book that are good for experienced genealogists as well.

If you are a more experienced genealogist, then you should consider picking up *The Troubleshooter's Guide to Do-It-Yourself Genealogy*. It is targeted toward those who have moved beyond the beginner's resources and search tactics and are beginning to hit some real stumbling blocks in their research. It provides you some sources you may not have been aware of, how to access them and how to get the most out of them.

Whether you are an experienced or beginning genealogist, you may benefit from any of the other titles in the *Quillen's Essentials of Genealogy* series, which provide more in-depth treatment on each topic:

• *Mastering Online Genealogy*
• *Mastering Census & Military Records*
• *Tracing Your European Roots*
• *Tracing Your Irish & British Roots*
• *Mastering Family, Library & Church Records*

Okay – so now that you're ready, let's strap on our genealogical seatbelts and find some of those immigrating ancestors of yours!

2. THE BASICS

Before we get too far along this genealogical journey we're taking together, let's take a few minutes and set the stage for searching for your immigrant ancestors. There are many records available to assist your research. I have found that it usually takes multiple records to yield the information I am looking for. One document sheds light in one area, which leads me to another, which confirms the previous data and provides me with more data. Tiny clues are left in countless records, clues that initially don't seem to be important, but which may later prove to be just the item of information needed to solve a mystery.

The goal, of course, is to find the genealogical information for your ancestors and their families. As you discover a birth date and place in immigration or naturalization records, those will lead you to the land of nativity of your ancestor. Further searches in the land of their nativity will likely confirm information reported on the immigration or naturalization record, uncover other family members, and assist you in moving further along on your pedigree chart, pushing it ever backward.

When searching for your immigrating ancestors, don't be in a rush to jump to immigration and naturalization records. There are many such records – that is true. But a little preparation on your part may help you go to the correct collections without first combing through collections that do not have records for your ancestors.

To be the most efficient in your search, first gather all the information you know about your ancestor. Speak with living parents, grandparents, aunts and uncles, cousins, etc. One of them may recall information that will become important to your search. Maybe they recall an ancestor who mentioned how beautiful Boston was when they stepped off the ship bringing them to America. Or perhaps they remember that great grandpa mentioned he had 3 lire in his pockets when he stepped off the ship in New York.

Do your US records homework before looking for immigration and naturalization records.

United States records first

Often, information that will help you in your search for immigrant ancestors will be information found in United States – not immigration, emigration or naturalization – records. A census record that lists your ancestor may list him or her under a name you didn't realize they went by. As an example, consider the following 1920 census record for my great grandparents:

My great grandmother was Theodora Charity McCollough, but the name she went by was Dolly. So a search of a census, immigration or naturalization record might not turn her up if I search for Theodora Charity Quillen. At a minimum, I should search under Theodora, Charity and Dolly. A death certificate, tombstone, obituary or other very US record may well reveal information I did not know, but information that will help me pinpoint her later on in other records.

The federal censuses for 1900, 1910, 1920, 1930 and 1940 each asks a series of questions that may provide clues that will assist you in finding these ocean-going (mountain-climbing, desert-crossing) ancestors of yours. These censuses all asked whether a person had been naturalized, along with other helpful immigration-related questions. The 1920 census went a step further by requesting the year of naturalization. That last will be especially helpful, and will assist you in locating your ancestors' naturalization papers. By census, here are the immigration and natural-ization questions asked:

1900
• If an immigrant, the year of immigration to the United States
• How long the immigrant has been in the United States
• Is the person naturalized

1910
• Year of immigration to the United States
• Whether naturalized or alien
• Whether able to speak English, or, if not, give language spoken

1920
• Year of immigration to the United States
• Naturalized or alien
• If naturalized, year of naturalization

1930
• Year of immigration into the United States
• Naturalization
• Whether able to speak English

1940 Census
• Citizenship of the foreign born
• Residence on April 1, 1935
• Mother tongue

In the Citizenship column of these censuses, where the above questions were asked, these abbreviations were used: AL = Alien, NA = Naturalized, NR = Not Reported, PA = First Papers filed (the immigrant's declaration of intent).

> Censuses may provide important clues to immigration and naturalization records.

What's in a name?

Further to the discussion above — do you know your ancestors' given as well as surnames? Knowing their given names – all of them – may help you sort out your ancestor from millions of others. Perhaps he or she went by a middle or christening name. While you might be unable to locate your ancestor Johannes Schmidt in records, you might discover a Wilhelm Schmidt who immigrated to the UnitedStates. Johannes Wilhelm Schmidt, like the author of this book, just happened to go by his middle name, not his first name.

As mentioned above in the example about my great grandmother, Theodora Charity Quillen, I'd do well to be open to diminutives as well as other possible nicknames as I scour records in search of her.

Know your history

Knowing a little of the history of your family as well as their native country may also help you pin down that immigrant ancestor of yours. If family tradition is that your second great grandfather came to America during the Great Potato Famine in Ireland, then that narrows your search for other records to a manageable half dozen years or so – 1845 to 1852. During that time period, a blight hit the potatoes of Ireland, rotting them in the ground. Potatoes were the main staple for the Irish diet, and it is estimated that approximately one million souls perished as a result. In addition, approximately another million Irish immigrated from Ireland during this time, the majority of which came to America.

One of my wife's ancestors is from Germany. Family tradition holds that as it looked like Germany was headed into what has become known as

History isn't just for the classroom. Learn the history of your ancestors' native lands.

The Great War (World War I), her second great grandmother packed her four military-age sons off to America to get them out of harm's way. That tells me I should search for their immigration records in the years leading up to the war's outbreak in 1914.

So – pay attention to history!

Be flexible

As a genealogist, people should be able to call you Ms. or Mr. Gumby when it comes to some things. One of those areas is the spelling of the surnames for which you are searching. Changes in the spellings of names happen, and I suppose the reasons for the changes are as endless and as intriguing as the individuals involved. Meier may have become Meyer, Schmidt might morph to Smith, Weiss becomes White and so on. It could be because of over-worked employees at immigration centers (as has often been alleged, although I am not sure that's true!), but it could also be for a myriad of other reasons, including the desire to become an American in every way possible, including the spelling of surnames. My family has a tradition that the spelling of our surname – Quillen – differs from other branches of the family (Quillan, Quillin, etc.) because after several generations of illiteracy a teacher asked some youngsters how they spelled their name. Not knowing, they accepted the teacher's spelling of Quillen. True? Legend? Who knows? The original Quillen to come to America was actually a McQuillan. He dropped the Mc from his name. I have come across members of the family who have added the Mc back after several hundred years.

So – be flexible when it comes to searching for names in US as well as immigration-related records. Because I wasn't as flexible as I should have been, it took me many years to locate my third- and fourth-great grandfathers in the US census. These gentlemen, though living next door to one another, found their names spelled differently – and neither correctly – on the 1860 US census for Lee County, Virginia:

Listed above are my twelve-year-old second great grandfather Jonathan Quillen (note both his given and surnames are misspelled – Johnathan Qulline), his father Frank Quillen (surname spelled Qulline) and his father – my fourth great grandfather – Leven Quillen (misspelled Leven Quilling). Because I wasn't flexible enough to consider (or at least pay attention to!) alternate spellings of the family surname, these significant records went unfound after many years of searching!

The same lessons apply to searching for your immigrant ancestors. Be flexible to alternate spellings of their last names. Sometimes accents were sufficiently thick to cause the problem, other times it was the enumerator's carelessness, or a host of other reasons.

Ethnic gatherings
Often, immigrants coming to America were coming to join other family members or neighbors. As you search for your immigrant ancestors, be

aware of where large populations of their ethnic group may have settled. Swedes ended up in Minnesota, the Irish centered in Boston and New York, the Polish in Chicago, Italians in New York and Chicago, even Bulgarians in New Mexico. (Bet you didn't know that!) While stereotypes or assumptions such as these may not apply to your ancestors, you cannot afford to overlook the possibility. Had I Irish ancestors (I do – lucky me!), I would be sure and search immigration records for Boston and New York. Could they have entered the US someplace else? Of course. But as a starting point, these ports of entry make the most sense if I have nothing better to go on.

Religion
You ask why religious affiliation should be considered? Well, because sometimes like-minded religionists immigrated to the US at the same time. Look at the founding of our country, which started with a colony of Pilgrims who came to America aboard the Mayflower, followed by the Puritans. Many early Pennsylvania pioneers were Quakers. If your ancestors came from Ireland, they're sure to be Catholic, right? Well, maybe – remember that the area that is now Northern Ireland was once "planted" by Queen Elizabeth with Protestants during the late 16th and 17th centuries (there's that history thing again!). Searching Catholic baptismal records for an ancestor from the northern counties of Ireland might prove fruitless.

I have used – and will continue to use throughout this book – the general term *immigration and naturalization records*. These terms, although often used together, indicate two distinct types of information:

Immigration records refer to those records that detail information about your ancestors' trip (immigration) to America. They include:

1. **Ship passenger lists** – these are the rosters of all who traveled on a particular ship to the United States. They are sometimes called *ship manifests*. These records, especially in later immigration years, contain a great deal of information of genealogical value.

2. **Certificates of arrival** – these were short notices containing the immigrant's name, date of departure and arrival, port of departure and entry and the name of the ship on which they traveled. Very little information of genealogical value is to be found on Certificates of Arrival, but they may lead you to other more helpful documents.

3. **Censuses** – censuses taken in later years after an immigrant's arrival may contain valuable clues to finding immigration and naturalization papers completed by the immigrant. The census itself is full of genealogical value, but may lead you to other documents that will expand that information exponentially.

4. **Emigration records** – these are records kept at the location where your ancestor embarked on a ship to come to America. Sometimes they provide significant information, sometimes they do not. Don't overlook them when searching for your immigrant ancestors.

Naturalization records refer to those records immigrants completed to become US citizens. There are several:

5. **Declarations of Intent** – these were papers completed to indicate the immigrant's intention to become a US citizen. They were often completed immediately upon arrival in the United States, but were sometimes completed later. These are often called *first papers*. These papers usually have a great deal of genealogical information in them.

6. **Petitions for Naturalization** – these papers were completed by the immigrant as part of his or her formal request to become a US citizen. Generally speaking, these could not be completed until an immigrant had been in the US at least five years. Also called *second papers* or *final papers*, as well as *Petition for Citizenship*. These papers usually have a great deal of genealogical information in them.

7. **Oaths of Allegiance** – this is the document the immigrant signs as s/he becomes a US citizen, renouncing their allegiance to any other

foreign power, dignitary, king, etc. Very little information of a genealogical value is contained in Oaths of Allegiance, but there may be some clues that will lead you to other sources of information.

Okay – now that we know the basics, we're ready to strap on our shoes and jump into our search for your immigrant ancestors.

3. A LITTLE HISTORY

Before we launch into tactics and learn about specific immigration and naturalization records, it would be wise for us to discuss the history of immigration in the United States. Doing so will give you a context that will aid your understanding of what records are available, when a national interest in keeping track of immigrants began, etc.

America is, first and foremost, a land of immigrants. Whether your ancestors trudged across the Bering Straits or up through South and Central America, whether from our neighbors to the north or from across the shining seas, our ancestors are all immigrants. Our discussion will start many years to the right of the timeline for when immigrants first started arriving on this big North American continent.

1776 – the birth of a new nation. 1789 — the ratification of our Constitution. The ink was barely dry on the Constitution when Congress passed the **Naturalization Act** in March 1790. This law provided for an orderly process for immigrants to become citizens of the United States.

The original Naturalization Act stipulated that anyone wanting to become a citizen of the United States must be a free white citizen who "... *behaved as a man of good moral character.*" In so doing, it prohibited indentured servants, free blacks, Asians and Indians. It also stipulated that naturalization was inherited through the father, whether or not he was a citizen (I guess they figured he had something to do with the birth).

The original Naturalization Act passed in 1790.

To prove that he had behaved as a man of good moral character, an immigrant had to have:

a) been in the United States at least two years, and

b) lived in the state from which he was applying for citizenship for at least one year, and

c) two witnesses who would attest to the immigrant's good moral character and residency. (I suppose they didn't have utility bills back then to prove residency…). Note – don't just blow past those who were witnesses. They were people who knew the immigrant well – often they were family members.

Once an immigrant met the above requirements, he or she could file a Petition for Naturalization with "…any common law court of record" that had jurisdiction over the area where the immigrant-soon-to-be-citizen lived. Courts of record include municipal, county, state or federal courts. Between this Act's passage and 1906, Petitions for Naturalization were filed with county, territorial, state or federal courts. This is an important piece of information for individuals seeking the naturalization papers for their ancestors who immigrated – or who requested naturalization – prior to 1906. It is a clue to where you need to search for your ancestor's naturalization documents.

> Prior to 1906, immigrants could file their naturalization papers with any common law court of record.

The Naturalization Act of 1790 was superseded by the Naturalization Act of 1795. This later Act extended residence requirement from two to five years – I guess someone figured it was more difficult to keep your nose clean for five years than for two years! It also provided a two-step process to becoming a citizen – adding the Declaration of Intent, followed by the Petition for Citizenship.

Further changes in the naturalization laws of this country occurred. As a result of the success of the Civil War, the Naturalization Act of 1870 extended citizenship to those of African descent born in the United States. Three decades later, a Supreme Court decision in 1898 granted citizenship to Asians when they granted citizenship to a child who was born in the United States to Chinese (non-citizen) parents.

Alas, with the responsibility of declaring naturalized citizenship resting with county, territorial, state and federal courts, for the first 116 years of naturalization in this country, there was no standardization of Petitions for Naturalization or questions on those petitions. So, in addition to their dispersion, there is also no standardization of the information you could expect to find when you do find a Petition. Some Petitions included the most basic of information, while others included significantly more – and often genealogical – information.

In 1906, the federal government stepped in and standardized the forms and the questions on the forms. Also, the records were now kept in federal government archives, many of which (along with earlier records) have been filmed and are now available at such genealogy sites as Ancestry. com, FamilySearch.org, and Fold3.com.

Other changes came along to impact the search for your ancestors. Up until 1922, immigrating women did not need to apply for citizenship unless they desired to. If they married a citizen, they gained citizenship. If their immigrant husband became a natu-ralized citizen, his wife and minority children also became citizens. Whether a requirement or not, many of the natu-ralization papers I have seen for women – usually Petitions for Citizenship or Declarations of Intent – list both the woman's married name and her maiden name, typically written like: *Catharine*

> In 1906 the federal government took over immigration and natu-ralization, standardizing forms and asking many genealogically significant questions.

Rose McQuillan nee Catharine Rose Murphy, or *Catharine Rose McQuillan, formerly Catharine Rose Murphy*. In those cases when only their married name was listed, later forms included a question about the name they arrived with – so in this case, had Catharine Rose been single when she arrived in the United States, she would have answered that she arrived under the name Catharine Rose Murphy.

Another change in the naturalization process occurred due to the Civil War. The North was desperately in need of fighting men, so legislation was passed that granted citizenship to any foreign-born male who served in the United States army and who was honorably discharged (there's that "good moral character" thing again!). The legislation waived the need for a Declaration of Intent, and the residency requirement was shortened from five years to one year. Many immigrants took advantage of this change in the naturalization process to expedite their citizenship, as well as to fight for their new country.

If such a book as *The History of the Greatest Ironies of the United States* existed, I am sure it would be noted that until 1924, most Indians – *Native Americans* – were not considered US citizens. In 1924, someone finally realized that Native Americans should have citizenship, so legislation was passed granting it to them. Before that time, some Indian women were citizens because they had married a white man – a citizen. Others gained citizenship because of serving in the military. A few Indians had become citizens because of special treaties. But until 1924, Indians, generally speaking, were not citizens. Then on June 2, 1924, the **Indian Citizenship Act** was passed by Congress and signed into law by Calvin Coolidge. The wording of the Act itself was short and sweet:

"BE IT ENACTED by the Senate and House of Representatives of the United States of America in Congress assembled, That all non-citizen Indians born within the territorial limits of the United States be, and they are hereby, declared to be citizens of the United States: Provided that the granting of such citizenship shall not in any manner impair or otherwise affect the right of any Indian to tribal or other property.

Note that last comment:

Provided that the granting of such citizenship shall not in any manner impair or otherwise affect the right of any Indian to tribal or other property.

Given the history of their dealings with white men, I am sure many Indians were concerned that granting of citizenship now meant something untoward was about to happen! I am sure this sentence was added to attempt to allay such fears!

Through the years and across jurisdictions, Petitions for Citizenship, Declarations of Intent and Oaths of Allegiance have changed and evolved. Until the federal government standardized the program, content of these documents varied, but the most general comment about those earlier forms is that they often contained the briefest of information: the name of the immigrant, date of his / her arrival in the United States, place from which they came and date of the document. Sometimes the entire document is handwritten, other times it is a fill-in-the-blank form. On the next page is a transcription of the Petition for Citizenship for James Taylor (no – not *The* James Taylor of rock-n-roll fame!).

James's handwritten petition provides information about his native land (Ireland), that he immigrated here when he was three years old, and has lived in the United States for "…twenty-three years and upward." Also note that he signed his name James Taylor Jr. – a clue to his father's name. Accompanying James's Petition was his Oath of Allegiance, which was witnessed by two individuals – one of which was William Taylor. Were I doing research on James, I would do well to make note that William Taylor may be a close relative – brother, son, uncle, cousin, etc.

United States
Western District of Pennsylvania

To the Honorable Judge of the Court of the United States, in and for the said district:

The petition of James Taylor of said district humbly showeth that said petitioner is a native of Ireland, and was heretofore a subject of the King of the United Kingdom of Great Britain and Ireland, that he has resided within the limits and under the jurisdiction of the United States of America twenty-three years and upwards, and in the state of Pennsylvania twenty-two years and upwards. That at the time of his arrival, that he was an Infant only three years of age, and that he has resided in the United States previous to the 14th of April, AD 1801. That he will support the Constitution of the United States, and that he does absolutely and entirely renounce all allegiance and fidelity to any foreign power, potentates or sovereigns whatever, and particularly to the King of the United Kingdom of Great Britain and Ireland whereof he was heretofore a subject. Your petitioner therefore prays that he may be admitted to become a Citizen of the United States of America.

James Taylor, Jr.

To illustrate the lack of standardization, I found another Petition for Citizenship from 1798 — four years prior to James's Petition. Unlike James's petition, this one was a fill-in-the-blank form – see next page. Note: It thrills me to review documents like this, that are over two hundred years' old!

Both petitions were made within the District Court for Pennsylvania, one for the Western District thereof. The information in the latter petition is even more scant than the first – the immigrant's name (Daniel McArthur), his former country of residence (Scotland), his current residence (Philadelphia) and the date of his application – June 29, 1798.

(I have bolded the parts that were handwritten / signed; the rest was pre-printed in an elegant script):

> To the Honorable **Richard Peters, Esquire, Judge of the United States for the District of Pennsylvania.**
>
> The Petition of **Daniel McArthur**, a native of **Scotland** but now of the **City of Philadelphia,**
>
> Respectfully Sheweth
>
> That he hath resided in the limits and under the jurisdiction of the United States for eleven years last past and upwards one year thereof within the state of Pennsylvania, where he was actually resident on the 29th day of January, 1795 — that he hath never born any heriditary title, or been of any of the orders of nobility, and that if he should by any means unknown to him, become entitled to any such, he doth hereby expressly renounce the same, and every claim and pretention thereto — that he wisheth to become a Citizen of the United States — he, therefore humbly prays, that on his taking the oath, making the proofs and complying with the requisites prescribed by law, he may be admitted to become a Citizen of the said United States.
>
> **Daniel McArthur**
>
> Philadelphia, **June 29th, 1798**
>
> **Daniel McArthur**, the foregoing petitioner, being duly sworn according to law, declareth and faith, that the facts contained in the foregoing petition are true.
>
> **Daniel McArthur**
>
> **Sworn in open court**

June 29, 1798
DC Alderwell, Deputy Clerk
John Wallington, *of the City of Philadelphia,* **Shoemaker**, *being duly sworn according to law, on his oath, declareth that he hath been acquainted with* **Daniel McArthur**, *the foregoing petitioner, for the space of two years now last past and upwards, and during all which time the petitioner* **Daniel McArthur** *hath to this* **deponent's** *knowledge behaved as a man of good moral character, attached to the Constitution of the United States and well disposed to the good order and happenings of the same.*

John Wallington

Sworn in open court
June 29, 1798
DC Alderwell, Deputy Clerk

Daniel McArthur, *the foregoing petitioner, being duly sworn according to law, on his oath, further declareth that he doth absolutely and entirely renounce and abjure all allegiance and fidelity to any foreign prince, potentates, state or sovereignty whatever, and particularly to the* **King of the United Kingdom of Great Britain and Ireland** *whereof he was heretofore a* **subject**, *and that he will support the Constitution of the United States.*

Daniel McArthur

Sworn in open court
June 29, 1798
DC Alderwell, Deputy Clerk

4. IMMIGRATION RECORDS

There are a number of records I would consider immigration records, versus naturalization records. The latter are those records used by the immigrant to apply for and eventually be granted citizenship in the United States. The former are records that have to do with the individual's immigration to and arrival in the US, including a number you might not consider immigration records.

The first immigration records we'll discuss are **Passenger Lists**. Passenger lists, also known as **Ship Manifests**, are the rosters of all passengers who traveled from a distant land to the United States. In and of themselves, they are – or can be – chock full of great genealogical information. One caution about passenger lists – virtually all the information on them, even though some of it may be of great genealogical value — is considered secondary source information. Birthdates, birth places, names of relatives, etc., are all secondary data. In some cases, the passenger list may be the only place that information exists, so it may be of great value. As you glean the information from the passenger lists, it may provide you with the clues you need to locate primary sources for that information.

For many years, these lists, although they existed, were not easily accessible to the public. However, in recent years, more and more of them have been finding their way online through the work of legions of volunteers. The LDS Church, genealogy societies from all over the world, and interested genealogists have made their mark in this genealogical area. (Thank you to all those involved in converting these records and placing them online!)

So just where do we find these records? *EllisIsland.org. Ancestry.com. Fold3.com. FamilySearch.org. CyndisList.org.* And a plethora of other websites across the width and breadth of the Internet. Many of those sites are subscription-based, while many others are free to the public. It goes without saying that not every resource has all the available passenger lists online. Some are stronger than others. Some focus on geographic regions of the US. Many novice genealogists believe – if they thought about it at all – that all immigrants to the United States came through Ellis Island. That is hardly the case. While a significant number did enter through her gates (over 12,500,000!), there were many other points of entry. Some experts on the topic estimate that well over 300 ports of entry were used by immigrants on their journey into the United States. But – the vast majority came through a handful of ports. Below is a list of the busiest immigrant ports between 1820 and 1920, along with the estimated number of immigrants processed:

Between 1820 and 1920, immigrants entered the US in the following numbers at the following points:

Baltimore, MD – 1,460,000
Boston, MA — 2,050,000
Charleston, SC – 20,000
Galveston, TX – 110,000
Key West, FL – 130,000
New Bedford, MA – 40,000
New York City, NY – 23,960,000 (Ellis Island and its predecessor Castle Garden)
New Orleans, LA – 710,000
Passamaquoddy, Maine – 80,000
Philadelphia, PA – 1,240,000
Portland / Falmouth, ME – 120,000
Providence, RI – 40,000
San Francisco, CA – 500,000

Given those numbers, the top ports in order of arrival in the United States were:

New York
Boston
Baltimore
Philadelphia
New Orleans
San Francisco

Those ports accounted for the processing of nearly 30 million immigrants over that 100-year period. That's a peck and two-thirds of immigrants! Passenger lists evolved over the history of the United States. Early passenger lists are just that – lists of those traveling on the ships. Prior to 1820, mostly you would find passenger lists that provide the name of the ship, date of arrival, port of arrival, and the name, age and country (sometimes the town also) of origin for the passenger (who may or may not have been an immigrant – they may have been traveling for business, to see family, etc.).

Beginning in 1820 and running through 1891, ship's captains were required to provide complete lists of their passengers to the Customs Collector (thank you, Mr. Taxman!). That's the good news. The bad news is that not all ports abided by this directive until 1905, but many did. Information on these passengers included their name, sex, age, occupation and native country. A *Remarks* column was on some ships' manifests. During this period also, the question: "Country in which they intend to become inhabitants" – is a helpful morsel of information. Prior to 1820, it was not common for children to appear on the passenger lists.

When passenger lists were standardized, there was typically more information.

In 1891 the responsibility for collecting this information transferred from the Customs Department to other departments within the federal government, eventually ending up with the Immigration and Naturalization Service (INS) in 1906. Along with these changes, came standardization of the forms and questions that were asked:

From 1893 to 1902, the following information was asked:

Name
Age
Marital status
Last residence
Final destination in US
Whether been to the US before
Name and address of relative or friend being joined, if any
Whether able to read and write
If they have a ticket to their final destination
Who paid for their ticket
Whether they were a polygamist or anarchist
Their health

In 1903, questions were added about their race.

In 1906, a personal description and birthplace were added.

In 1907, they began asking for the name and address of the closest living relative in their native country.

As you can see, as the years went by, more information important to genealogists was asked. Now let's talk about a couple of my favorite websites for exploring passenger lists:

www.EllisIsland.org. I am particularly fond of this website. I think those responsible for this project did a fine job of making passenger lists accessible to the public of all those who entered America through the gates of *Isola della Lacrime* – The Island of Tears – as dubbed by Italian immigrants. The Ellis Island website is free to the public, although you must register to use it. There is no cost – they just like to keep track of those who are visiting. I have received very few e-mails from them through the years, so don't worry about being spammed when you provide your e-mail address.

Ellis Island was open from 1892 until 1924, and their website contains information on about 12.5 million immigrants who came through her gates.

The website is pretty straight-forward: on the first page, you enter the name of the person you are seeking. At least the surname of the person you are seeking is required, although you can also add an approximate birth date if you like and if you know it, to narrow your search results. If you add a birth date and nothing comes up, remove the birth date and see what happens. As with any website, if you get too fine in your search terms, you are liable to miss your ancestor. For example, if your great grandfather Jimmy McQuillan came through Ellis Island and you look for him under that name, you might not get any hits. If not, try James McQuillan, Jim McQuillan, J. McQuillan, or simply go with Mc-Quillan, then weed through the non-James's to see if you can find him.

Once you enter the name of your ancestor, you'll be rewarded with a list of all those included in the Ellis Island passenger lists who match that name. For example, I entered the name of a shirt-tail relative of mine, Elizabeth McQuillan, and received the following result:

MATCHING PASSENGER RECORDS

Name of Passenger	Residence	Arrived	Age on Arrival
Elizabeth McQuillan	Clydebank, Scotland	1923	50
Elizabeth McQuillan	Coleraine, Ireland	1922	20

I select the first Elizabeth and click on the *View Ship Manifest* choice, and I am taken to a transciption of the ship's manifest. If I wish (you should), I can also look at the original ship's manifest. When you select that at the top of the page, you'll see a very small picture of the ship's manifest – about 3" x 4". Now, I don't know about you, but that's a little small for me. Never fear – look for the small magnifying glass icon on the right-hand side and click that. You'll be rewarded with a much larger – and more legible — page.

Scanning the passenger list, I immediately see Elizabeth McQuillan and three sons on lines 13 through 16:

McQuillan, Elizabeth
McQuillan, John
McQuillan, Patrick
McQuillan, James

U. S. DEPARTMENT OF LABOR
IMMIGRATION SERVICE

List _____ 19

LIST OR MANIFEST OF ALIEN PASSENGERS FOR THE UNITED

ALL ALIENS arriving at a port of continental United States from a foreign port or a port of the insular possessions of the United States, and all aliens arriving at a port of said insular possessions from a foreign port, a port of continental United States or a port of another insular possession. This (white) sheet is for the listing of

S. S. _____ *Passengers sailing from* Southampton _____ , October 20, 1923, 19

No. on List.	HEAD-TAX STATUS	NAME IN FULL — Family name	Given name	Age Yrs. Mos.	Sex	Married or single	Calling or occupation	Able to — Read / Read what language / Write	Nationality Yes/Wm.	Race or people	Last permanent residence Country / City or town	The name and complete address of nearest relative or friend in country whence alien came.	Final destination State / City or town
1		McDonall	William		M S	Confectr.	yes English	Scotland	Scotch	Scotland	Greenock	Mother: Margret McNail, 33 Brougham Street, Greenock.	Mich. Flint
2		McNeill	James Roger		M S	Waiter	"	Scotland	"	"	"	Mother: Margret McNail, 32 Brougham Street, Greenock.	" Flint
3		McNae	James		M S	Draper	"	England	English	England	Barrow	Father: Daniel McNeal, 4 Penrith Place, Barrow.	"
4		McNae	Sarah		F S	Cigar maker	"	Scotland	"	Scotland	Glasgow	Father: 264 Thistle Street, Glasgow.	Pa. Phila.
5		McNae	Catherine		F S	Servant	"	"	"	"	"	Father:	"
6		MacPherson	Hugh Margaret		F M	H/wife	"	Scotland	Irish	"	Greenock	Sister: Mrs. MacCabon, 2 Dougall Street, Greenock.	Pa.
7		MacPherson	Katie		F S	Student	"	"	"	"	"	aunt:	"
8		MacPherson	Peggie		F S	Child	"	"	"	"	"	"	"
9		MacPherson	Lachlan		M S	"	"	"	"	"	"	"	"
10		MacPherson	Junior			S	Infant	"	"	"	"	"	"	"
11		MacPherson	Matthew		M S	Brass moulder	"	"	"	"	"	Mother: Mrs. E. McPherson, 410 Baltic Street, Glasgow.	"
12		MacPherson	Katherine		F S	Domestic	"	"	"	"	Greenock	Mrs. Wm. Pherson, 31 Ladyburn Bldgs. Greenock.	"
13		McQuillan	Elizabeth		F M	Wife	"	"	"	"	Clydebank	Son: William McQuillan, 7 Clyde St. Clydebank.	N.Y. Brooklyn
14		McQuillan	John		M S	"	"	"	"	"	"	Brother:	"
15		McQuillan	Patrick		M S	"	"	"	"	"	"	"	"
16		McQuillan	James		M S	Plumber	"	"	"	"	Paisley	Wife: Mrs. Lily Ross, 21 George St. Paisley.	Pa. Phila.
17		McNae	Robert		M S	Plumber	"	"	"	"	Glasgow	Mother: 65 Dumas Street, Bridgeton, Gla. agon.	
18		McNae	Edmund		M S	Laborer	"	"	"	"	"	"	"

The top of this ship's manifest provides me important information about this family – the ship on which they traveled (Leviathan), their port of departure (Southampton, England), and the date they departed (October 20, 1923). Later in the *Naturalization Records* section, you'll learn that several of the naturalization documents completed by immigrants listed the name of the ship in which they sailed to America, as well as the date they arrived and their port of entry. The Ellis Island website also allows you to search first by ship, then by the surname of the traveling immigrant.

A caution about the Ellis Island website: sometimes it feels like you may be entering the passenger list in the middle – there are no names on the left, but answers running to the right. It is because you did in fact enter in the middle of the record. In later years, the passenger lists covered two facing pages; what you have done is entered on page 2 of your immigrant ancestor's listing. Just go back one page and you'll be able to start. Note the line number on which your ancestor's record is found, and when you return to the second page, you'll be able to glean more information.

Be sure and look for page 2 of the ship's passenger lists.

On the page I have listed above, a tremendous amount of information is available for Elizabeth McQuillan. Here's a sampling of that which is genealogically useful:

— she is 50 years old
— she is traveling with three children: John (17), Patrick (15) and James (9)
— she is married (but where is her husband!?)
— she is from Scotland, and is Scottish (note the number on this page that are from Scotland but are Irish – the Irish often left Ireland to work in Scotland and England)
— her son – William McQuillan – is her nearest relative in the country from which she came
— her final destination is Brooklyn, New York

The second page of the ship's manifest (which I have not included), tells me the following information:

— she had $22 in her pockets when she arrived
— her (and her children's) fare was paid for by her husband — she and her children were going to meet her husband, Adam McQuillan, and his address in Brooklyn was listed
— whether she had been to the United States or not (she nor her children had been here before)
— she and her children intended to be here permanently (that is – they were immigrating and not just visiting)
— she and her children intended to become citizens
— she was not a polygamist or anarchist (!)
— she was in good health
— she was 5'-2" tall, had a fresh complexion and brown hair
— she and her oldest two children were born in Glasgow, Scotland
— her youngest child, James, was born in Clydebank, Scotland

As you can see, this passenger list has provided a boat-load (no pun intended…well, maybe a little) of genealogical information.

Be sure and remember this family. We will use them to illustrate various other sources of information that can be found for your immigrant ancestors.

Now – I don't want you to get too excited. While the information for Elizabeth and her children is something to get excited about, not all ship's manifests / passenger lists are this complete. In the early decades / centuries of keeping immigration records, just like the censuses, the information collected was very sparse, then developed more and more through the years. Had Ms. McQuillan immigrated 100 years earlier, it is probable that the most we would have gotten for her from the passenger list would have been her name, port of departure and port of entry, and dates associated with each. If lucky, we may have gotten her birth date.

It is a 50-50 proposition as to whether her children would have been listed in the earlier records. For now, let's be happy that as time went on, the list of questions and information kept on each immigrant grew and took on a more genealogical focus.

Bottom line: Ellisisland.org = great website!

www.Castlegarden.org – Castle Garden was the immigration processing, New York port of arrival predecessor to Ellis Island. While Ellis Island processed 12.5 million immigrants, Castle Garden was no slacker – processing over 11 million immigrants during the seventy-two years their doors were open – from 1820 to 1892. From 1855 to 1890 it was America's first official immigration center. It is estimated that over 100 million Americans – one in three – can trace at least one of their ancestors through either Castle Garden or Ellis Island. That's a lot of ancestors!

> Don't forget Ellis Island's predecessor – Castle Garden. Many records available

Whereas the records on Ellis Island's website are all digitized and online, those at Castle Garden are not yet, though they are working feverishly to make that happen. In the meantime, they have transcribed (as of this writing) nearly all their records, and they are available for you to view free of charge. After clicking the *Search*, you'll see this screen:

AMERICA'S FIRST
IMMIGRATION CENTER

Enter as much information as known. Use * as a wildcard.

SHIP	
PORT OF DEPARTURE	
FIRST NAME	
LAST NAME	
OCCUPATION	
COUNTRY OF LAST RESIDENCE	
PROVINCE OF LAST RESIDENCE	
PLACE OF LAST RESIDENCE	
DATE	1820 ▼ - 1913 ▼

SEARCH NOW

Complete it with the most information you have on your immigrant ancestor. Remember, however, that too much information might cause you to miss your ancestor. As mentioned earlier, Jimmy McQuillan might not be listed in the passenger lists as Jimmy, but as Jim, or James, or simply J. So be careful in how much information you enter. I usually start large (e.g. – McQuillan) and work it smaller.

Here's an example: Let's say I am searching for my long-lost ancestor, Catherine McQuillan. I know she came to America in the 1840s, but I don't want to eliminate some other dates, so I just decide to enter *Catherine McQuillan*. Here are the results:

SEARCH RESULTS   Results 1 - 1 of 2 Pages: « 1 of 1 »

LAST NAME▲	FIRST NAME	AGE	SEX	ARRIVAL DATE	PLACE OF LAST RESIDENCE
MCQUILLAN	CATHERINE	23	F	1 Apr 1848	U
MCQUILLAN	CATHERINE	50	F	2 Jan 1851	U

But what if I just enter McQuillan? Here's what I get:

SEARCH RESULTS   Results 1 - 20 of 116 Pages: « 1 of 6 »

LAST NAME▲	FIRST NAME	AGE	SEX	ARRIVAL DATE	PLACE OF LAST RESIDENCE
MCQUILLAN	PAT.	22	M	11 Apr 1856	U
MCQUILLAN	BRIDGET	21	F	9 Jun 1846	U
MCQUILLAN	CATH.	24	F	25 Jun 1848	BELFAST
MCQUILLAN	GEORGE	20	M	25 Jun 1848	BELFAST
MCQUILLAN	JOHN	20	M	27 Mar 1846	U
MCQUILLAN	CATHE	25	F	4 Nov 1846	U
MCQUILLAN	ANN	19	F	25 Apr 1846	U
MCQUILLAN	BRYAN	36	M	25 Apr 1846	U
MCQUILLAN	DMARGARETT	1	F	25 Apr 1846	U
MCQUILLAN	MARY	21	F	25 Apr 1846	U
MCQUILLAN	U	25	F	25 Apr 1846	U
MCQUILLAN	HENERY	8	M	15 May 1848	DERRY
MCQUILLAN	ROBERT	16	M	15 May 1845	DERRY
MCQUILLAN	CATHARINE	22	F	14 Jul 1846	U
MCQUILLAN	JOHN	20	M	14 Jul 1846	U
MCQUILLAN	MARY JANE	24	F	14 Jul 1846	U
MCQUILLAN	JANE	25	F	20 Jul 1846	U
MCQUILLAN	JAS	20	M	26 Jun 1847	U
MCQUILLAN	CATHERINE	23	F	1 Apr 1848	U
MCQUILLAN	JAMES	25	M	1 Apr 1848	U

Aha! My first effort, where I entered *Catherine McQuillan*, yielded two individuals total. On my second effort, where I entered only *McQuillan*, I received 116 McQuillans on six pages of results, and on the first page, I see four individuals whose name is probably Catherine. Yes, I have more pages to review (six, in this example), but that's a small price to pay to make sure I don't overlook my dear Catherine McQuillan.

Fortunately, the Castle Garden website allows the use of a wildcard, so I can try it again, typing C* McQuillan. When I do that, I get the following:

SEARCH RESULTS   Results 1 - 1 of 12 Pages: « 1 of 1

LAST NAME ▲	FIRST NAME	AGE	SEX	ARRIVAL DATE	PLACE OF LAST RESIDENCE
MCQUILLAN	CATH.	24	F	26 Jun 1848	BELFAST
MCQUILLAN	CATHE	25	F	4 Nov 1846	U
MCQUILLAN	CATHARINE	22	F	14 Jul 1846	U
MCQUILLAN	CATHERINE	23	F	1 Apr 1848	U
MCQUILLAN	CATH.	49	F	22 Jan 1848	U
MCQUILLAN	CATH.	0 m	F	17 Nov 1848	U
MCQUILLAN	CATHN.	30	F	4 May 1849	U
MCQUILLAN	CATHRINE	17	F	28 May 1850	U
MCQUILLAN	CATHERINE	50	F	2 Jan 1851	U
MCQUILLAN	CATHR.	14	F	20 Sep 1851	U
MCQUILLAN	CATHR.	40	F	20 Sep 1851	U
MCQUILLAN	CHARLES	15	M	15 Nov 1851	U

Now, this is a little more manageable. Of these twelve individuals, eleven are probably Catherine (or one of her various spellings). This listing includes all the Catherines that were to be found on the previous two efforts. (But what if she spelled her name with a K? Don't overlook that possibility!)

Once you have located one of the individuals to whom you think you may be related, click on her name, and you'll be taken to a transcription of the passenger list that her name appears on.

CATH. MCQUILLAN			
FIRST NAME	CATH.	RELATIVE LEFT BEHIND	
LAST NAME	MCQUILLAN	NAME OF RELATIVE LEFT BEHIND	
OCCUPATION	WIFE	ADDRESS OF RELATIVE LEFT BEHIND	
AGE	24	TICKET	
SEX	Female	PAID BY	Self
LITERACY	Unknown	IN THE US BEFORE	Unknown
SHIP	GRAMPION	IN THE US WHEN	
ARRIVED	26 Jun 1945	IN THE US WHERE	
COUNTRY	IRELAND	GOING TO SOMEONE IN THE US	Unknown
PORT OF DEPARTURE	BELFAST	RELATIONSHIP TO THAT SOMEONE IN THE US	
PLACE OF LAST RESIDENCE	BELFAST	NAME OF RELATIVE IN THE US	
PROVINCE OF LAST RESIDENCE	UNKNOWN		
CITY OR VILLAGE OF DESTINATION	UNITED STATES	ADDRESS OF RELATIVE IN THE US	
PLAN	Unknown	CITY OF RELATIVE IN THE US	
PASSAGE	Unknown	COUNTRY OF BIRTH	IRELAND
MONEY		PLACE OF BIRTH	

While I enjoy seeing the actual ship's manifests (passenger lists) available on EllisIsland.org, through the Castle Garden website, I have another 11 million transcribed records available to me. Not a bad deal!

Ancestry.com
Ancestry.com has been busy digitizing a great many passenger lists. As of this writing, Ancestry.com boasts these passenger list collections:

— Baltimore passenger lists, 1820-1872
— Baltimore passenger lists, 1892-1948
— Boston passenger lists, 1820-1943
— Hamburg passenger lists, 1850-1934
— Irish passenger lists, 1803-1806 and 1847-1871
— New Orleans passenger lists, 1820-1850
— New York passenger lists, 1820-1850, 1851-1891, 1935-1938
— Passenger list index, 1500-1900
— Philadelphia passenger lists, 1883-1945
— UK incoming passenger lists, 1878-1960

— New South Wales, Australia passenger lists, 1826-1922
— Vancouver, BC passenger lists (Chinese arrivals) – 1906-1912

…and another 445 such collections in their vast data warehouse! I hesitate providing the number of passenger lists. It seems that at least weekly I receive notification that Ancestry has added this or that collection. Passenger lists contain the names and (often) genealogical information for many people, and Ancestry.com is busy digitizing those and getting them online for those of us who are searching!

Ancestry.com is a subscription service, but it is available at many public libraries and LDS Family History Centers.

While Ancestry.com is a subscription service, it is available for free at any of the National Archives and Records Administration (NARA) facilities. It is also available for free at many public libraries, as well as many of the LDS church's local Family History Centers.

Following are other organizations, websites, and resources for passenger lists:

National Archives and Records Administration (NARA)
The National Archives (NARA) has immigration lists from 1820 through 1982 on microfilm, and many of them are available online through subscription services like Ancestry.com and Fold3.com. The records available at NARA are arranged by port of arrival. You can go to *www.archives.gov/research/immigration/index.html* to learn more about what is available through NARA, but here is a summary:

— Immigration records are kept by port of entry into the United States.
— Microfilmed copies of passenger lists up to 1955 are available at the National Archives in Washington DC, and some may be available at regional NARA locations. A link from the NARA site will take you to their microfilm catalog so you can see whether certain passenger list microfilms are available at one of the regional facilities.

If you aren't close enough to a regional NARA facility to visit personally, you can order copies of passenger arrival records by using order form NATF 81, or by ordering online. In addition, the information contained about various passenger lists will let you know whether those records are available online (most are not yet available through NARA) through some other subscription service, such as Ancestry.com and Fold3.com.

From the NARA website, you can search the various ports of entry to see what records they have, and to also see what facilities have copies of the microfilmed records. Many records can be found at any of NARA's fourteen regional facilities, while others are located at only

Ship passenger records may be available through ordering or visiting regional NARA facilities.

selected facilities. NARA's regional facilities are located in the following locations, along with contact information:

Anchorage, Alaska, e-mail: alaska.archives@nara.gov
Website: www.archives.gov/pacific-alaska/anchorage/index.html

Laguna Niguel, California, e-mail: laguna.archives@nara.gov
Website: www.archives.gov/pacific/laguna/index.html

San Bruno, California, e-mail: sanbruno.archives@nara.gov
Website: www.archives.gov/pacific/san-francisco/index.html

Denver, Colorado, e-mail: denver.archives@nara.gov
Website: www.archives.gov/rocky-mountain/index.html

Morrow, Georgia, e-mail: atlanta.center@nara.gov
Website: www.archives.gov/southeast/index.html

Chicago, Illinois, e-mail: chicago.archives@nara.gov
Website: www.archives.gov/great-lakes/contact/directions-il.html

Waltham, Massachusetts, e-mail: waltham.center@nara.gov
Website: www.archives.gov/northeast/boston/

Pittsfield, Massachusetts, e-mail: archives@pittsfield.nara.gov
Website: www.archives.gov/northeast/boston/

Kansas City, Missouri, e-mail: kansascity.archives@nara.gov
Website: www.archives.gov/facilities/mo/kansas_city.html

New York, New York, e-mail: newyork.archives@nara.gov
Website: www.archives.gov/northeast/nyc/

Philadelphia, Pennsylvania, e-mail: philadelphia.archives@nara.gov
Website: www.archives.gov/midatlantic/agencies/

Fort Worth, Texas, e-mail: ftworth.archives@nara.gov
Website: www.archives.gov/southwest/index.html

Seattle, Washington, e-mail: seattle.archives@nara.gov
Website: www.archives.gov/pacific-alaska/seattle/index.html

Washington DC, Website: www.archives.gov/

Remember a few pages ago we searched for Catherine McQuillan on the Castle Garden website? Well, NARA does have some of their collection transcribed and available online. I decided to look for a Catharine McQuillan in the NARA records. I went to their main immigration records page at *www.archives.gov/research/immigration/index.html*, then near the bottom clicked on *Irish Famine Passenger Records in the Access to Archives Databases* (I think that's government-speak for: these records are available to look at online!) The description tells me that the database contains the passenger records for over 600,000 people who arrived in New York during the Irish Famine years of 1846 to 1851. It hastens to say that some 30% listed their native country as other than Ireland (thirty-two other countries are included in this group).

I discovered that if I used a wildcard on the NARA site, I had to include at least three letters of the name. So in Catherine's case, I couldn't use C* — I had to use Cat*. When I did, the information that was available online is shown in the table on the next page.

If you compare this list with the one a few pages back, it's comforting to see that each Catherine and her variant spellings are represented. The column that says *Manifest Identification Number* lists the name of each ship (even though *Guy Mannering, Isaac Webb*, etc., sound more like ship's masters than the actual names of ships!).

Last Name	First Name	Age	Native Country	Destination	Port of Embarkation	Passenger Arrival Date
McQuillan	Cathrine	17	Ireland	New York	Liverpool	5/28/1850
McQuillan	Cathr.	40	Gr. Britain	USA	Liverpool	9/20/1851
McQuillan	Cathn.	14	Gr. Britain	USA	Liverpool	9/20/1851
McQuillan	Cathr.	30	Ireland	USA	Liverpool	5/4/1849
McQuillan	Catherine	50	Ireland	USA	Liverpool	1/02/1851
McQuillan	Cath.	24	Ireland	USA	Liverpool	6/26/1848
McQuillan	Cath.	Born at sea	Ireland	USA	Liverpool	11/17/1848
McQuillan	Catherine	23	Ireland	USA	Liverpool	04/1/1848
McQuillan	Cathe.	25	Ireland	USA	Liverpool	11/4/1846
McQuillan	Cathr.	22	Gr. Britain	USA	Liverpool	07/14/1846
McQuillan	Cath.	49	Ireland	USA	Liverpool	01/22/1848

While the data provided here isn't as extensive as some other records, it provides several important bits of information: the port of entry (New York), the individual's native country, the ship they came on, and their arrival date. These will be important records for (hopefully!) finding naturalization records that might provide a little more genealogical information for your ancestors. (Note: while only one of the *Destination* designations says New York, these lists were in the New York Passenger Lists collection at NARA.)

Some websites allow the use of wild cards in searching for ancestors.

So – the good news is that here and there on the NARA website, you can find records that have been made available online – or at least transcriptions, like these. I have had some luck finding a few *Alien Enemy Registration* forms there also (you'll learn about them in the *Naturalization* section).

So far, all of the sources for passenger records I have presented are online. I know that there are many who can still stand to use *books* to glean information. One of the best – if not THE best — on the topic of passenger lists is *Passenger and Immigration Lists Index, 1500s to 1900s,* compiled by William Filby and published by Gale Research. For many years, especially prior to the digitization of these records, it was the Bible for genealogists to use. And for passenger lists prior to 1820, it may be a very valuable resource for you to procure, either as a purchase or at your local library. It is updated annually and is a great resource for researchers combing through passenger lists.

The book has compiled passenger lists, as the name indicates, between the 1500s and 1900s for those arriving in Canadian and US ports. The pages are close print in fine font (think phone book pages) with a ton of information and names! It boasts nearly 5 million entries for immigrants primarily from Britain, Ireland, Germany, France, Switzerland, and other European countries. Entries in the book include individual's name(s), age, place and year of arrival, the source of the information, and a page number where the information was found in the source. Families are gathered together. Women are listed by both their maiden name as well as their married name, if both were listed in the passenger list. Men are listed by all their given names. So, William Daniel Quillen would be found under William Quillen as well as Daniel Quillen.

Even though it is a book, if you prefer the online version, you can find the index at Ancestry.com at *search.ancestry.com/search/db.aspx?dbid=7486*. Mr. Filby and whoever he has had helping him through the years, used every imaginable source as he compiled these indexes. Thousands of different records were used, including ship's manifests, personal diaries and about anything else you can imagine. All are well documented in the *Source* section.

Check out Filby's book: *Passenger and Immigration Lists Index.*

Once you find an ancestor in Filby's book, you may want to see if you can find the original source as identified by Mr. Filby, as that source may have additional information about your ancestor.

Border-Crossing records
You say your ancestor didn't sail to America in a ship? You suspect he or she walked / rode a horse / drove a wagon across the border? Beginning in the late 19th century, the same kind of records were kept for these immigrants as were kept for those who arrived by ship. Similar questions were asked of travelers as they entered the country as were asked of travelers / immigrants entering our borders via ships. These records sometimes carried the title *List or Manifest of Alien Passengers Applying for Admission to the United States from Foreign Contiguous Territory*. So if your ancestors were French Canadians who came to the United States, these are records that would be important to check. Ancestry.com has a nice collection, and if you Google *Canadian border crossing records* you will find a number of websites that address this topic. Some will lead you almost immediately to subscription sites, while others provide infor-

mation for free. Records of immigrants from Canada began being kept in 1895. Some records – such as Customs records – were kept in the years previous to that.

Border-crossing records from Mexico began to be kept in 1906. Sometimes, instead of using the above-mentioned *List or Manifest of Alien Passengers*, immigration authorities chose not to collect arrival information quite the same as was collected for ship's passengers. Instead, they collected cards, called "card manifests," for each immigrant. These cards contained the same information as that collected on traditional ship passenger arrival lists, such as full name, age, sex, marital status, occupation, point of arrival in the United States, and final destination. The use of these cards was especially true in the border crossings between the US and Mexico. As time went on and the number of questions increased, the *List or Manifest of Alien Passengers* came into more general usage, both for Canadian as well as Mexican immigrants.

Sometimes, these older records, while not being standardized, also provided additional information. I was researching Canadian Border Crossing records on Ancestry.com, when I came across this transcribed record:

> **Name**: John Smith
> **Marital Status**: Married with four children
> **Year of record**: 1774
> **Comments**: Left the country week of 7th to 14th March; embarked from the Port of Hull bound for Fort Cumberland, North America on the vessel *Albion*, Master Thomas Perrot; former residence Yorkshire; purpose "…their Rents being raised by his Landlord Mr. Chapman they have made a purchase of some land in North America…"; child of Nathaniel and Elizabeth Smith
> Reference: Transcribed from original documents held in the collection of the National Archives of Canada [Ottawa]: MG 15, T.47, vol. 9, parts 1 and 2; page 6

Source: Treasury Registers - Weekly Emigration Returns 1773-1775 Extracts. An Account of all Persons who have taken their Passage on Board any Ship or Vessel, to go out of this Kingdom from any Port in England.

I am certain John Smith and his wife had no idea when they rebelled against Mr. Chapman's raised rent, that their plight would be reported almost 250 years later in a genealogy book!

Not all immigrants to the United States came on ships to America. Check border crossing records.

A small percentage of these border-crossing records have been digitized and are available online, or even transcribed and available online. Many records are available through the federal government's National Archives and Records Administration (NARA) website at *www.archives.gov/research/arc/index.html*. Once on their website, enter the information you are seeking – a surname or the type information you seek: *Mexico border crossing records*, for example. You will likely discover that information you are seeking is available on microfilm at one of NARA's fourteen national archive sites around the country. If you are fortunate, the details on the record will tell you that they have been digitized by Ancestry.com, Fold3. com or some other entity. As NARA does their own digitizing, those records will be available under the tab on the page that says *Digitized Copies* – happy day when you find those, although still a very small percentage of NARA's holdings have been digitized, either by them or by other organizations such as Ancestry.com or Fold3.com.

United States Customs Passenger Lists
From 1820 until about 1891, shipmasters were required to file their ship manifests with the customs office in each port in which they landed. During these years, the minimum information required of the ship masters was the name of the ship, her captain / master, its ports of embarkation and entry and dates of its departure and arrival. Information about the

ship's passengers included name, age, sex, occupation, nationality, country of origin and their intended destination. No standard government forms existed during this time, so formats varied widely according to the good will and pleasure of the shipmaster.

FamilySearch.org and the LDS Church

The LDS Church launched FamilySearch.org in 1999, and it immediately became one of the leading websites for family history research in the world. At last count, it was receiving more than 14 million hits per day, and is incredibly busy! It serves as a gateway to the incredibly vast genealogical collections of the LDS Church. Many of those records are available online – more and more each day, in fact. A still greater number are available via microfilm. Don't have a microfilm reader at home? That's okay. The LDS Church has some 4,500+ Family History Centers – small branches of their immense Salt Lake City-based Family History Library – where microfilms can be sent. The cost is minimal – $5.50 per roll to cover shipping – and they will remain in your local Family History Center for six weeks, where you can go and view them.

I can borrow microfilms from the LDS Church for six weeks. They can be delivered to a local LDS chapel or a public library.

The Family History Library has over 12,000 microfilm rolls of passenger lists that can be ordered and viewed. Just go to *www.familysearch.org*, then under *Browse by Location, click Europe (or Africa, Australia, New Zealand,* etc.). Then click on the country for which you are hoping to find passenger lists. In the box provided, type in passenger lists and see if FamilySearch has a collection that includes passenger lists addressing the location for which you are looking.

Immigrant Servants Database – *www.immigrantservants.com*

I have to admit, this is a pretty cool database, containing the names of more than 23,000 indentured servants, and information about each of them. Between 1607 and 1820, approximately 75 percent of the immigrants who came to the new world south of the New England area financed their voyage here by becoming one type of servant or another, including indentured servants and a class called redemptioners. A database containing the names and information about each of these 23,000+ servants can be found at the Immigrant Servants Database website at *www.immigrantservants.com*. Following is a typical listing that you'll find on this database:

Name
Surname: Murphy
Given Name: Edward
Soundex Code: M610

Birth, Christening and Other Information
Gender: Male
Nation: Ireland
Orphan: Unknown
Position in Parent's Family: Unknown
Landowner: Unknown
Literate: Unknown
Convict: Unknown

Place of Arrival
Ship: *William*

Length of Indenture
Year of Indenture: 1746
Length: 4 years

Place of Indenture
County: Chester
Colony: Pennsylvania

Agent
Surname: Daxon

Given name: Burton

Master
Surname: Flower
Given name: Samuel

> My ancestor may have been an indentured servant – check out *www.immigrantservants. com.*

If you don't find any relatives here, revisit the website every now and then – it is an ongoing project, and names are being added all the time.

Old Newspapers

You may ask, "You consider old newspapers as immigration records?" And my answer would be an emphatic "Yes!" As you search for some of your immigrant ancestors, you will absolutely insist they must have been teleported here, as they would have been had they been passengers or crew of the *USS Enterprise* of Star Trek fame! Or – for those of this newer generation – perhaps they arrived via port key, floo powder or simply apparated, as Harry Potter and his friends have been known to travel.

Despite your best efforts, you seem unable to find your ancestor on a passenger list, emigration list, naturalization papers, etc. – they just seem to have appeared one day. (Kind of gives credence to the arrival methods mentioned in the last paragraph.) Well, newspapers may help you locate these individuals and find additional clues as to when they arrived. Consider for a moment the following:

Obituaries will often have information about immigrant ancestors. You may have come up empty in your searches of passenger lists, naturalization papers, etc. Then you decide to look at newspapers from the small community where your ancestor lived. Note this obituary on the next page from the Grand Forks (North Dakota) Herald, November 4, 1893:

> Mrs. Nancy Huston died Nov. 23 in the 76th year of her age, after three years of intense suffering. She was a native of Ireland whence she imigrated to Pennsylvania in the early forties. She came with her family to North Dakota eight years ago and located near Bachelor's Grove. She was greatly beloved by all her neighbors and idolized by her household. She was buried near her late residence. Her husband, four sons and two daughters mourn her loss. The funeral services were conducted Nov. 25 by Rev. R. J. Creswell.

We learn from her obituary that Mrs. Huston immigrated from Ireland to Pennsylvania (check the Philadelphia passenger lists!) in the early (18)40s. That gives you a good starting point from which to search for other immigration and naturalization records. Knowing Irish history as you do, you may suspect that she came a little later, as a result of the Great Potato Famine in Ireland, 1845 to 1852. Since Nancy lived in North Dakota at the time of her death, you might have looked in Canadian border-crossing records for her, or been at a loss as to which port of entry she may have arrived. This may be a clue that helps you break through that conundrum.

Business pages sometimes will carry articles about local prominent businessmen and women, office-holding individuals, etc. They will often mention immigration information about the subject of their article. Consider this sample on the next page from *The Rockford (Illinois) Register*, from July 25, 1916. This article on Mr. James Carmichael of Ogle County, Illinois tells us he immigrated to America when he was three months old. Earlier in the article they give his age as 67, and since the article was written in 1916, you should begin your search of immigration records beginning around 1849 in Philadelphia (which port of entry the article also conveniently provided!). Look for the Robert and Jane Carmichael family with a three-month-old infant along for the ride. Irish emigration records might also be checked, as well as birth and christening records in Donegal, Ireland. (Hmmm – note the date of immigration for this Irish family – 1849. Another little family unit fleeing the starvation of Ireland?)

> The writer found much pleasure in a short visit with James Carmichael, owner and manager of Maplehurst stock farm, an excellent farm, located two miles from Lindenwood and seven miles north of Rochelle. Mr. Carmichael is one of the early pioneers of Ogle county a gentleman held in high esteem throughout the county. Mr. Carmichael was born in County Donegal, Ireland, sixty-seven years ago. In order to better their worldly condition, his parents, Robert and Jane Carmichael, imigrated to the United States, which to them was a veritable Land of Promise, when James was but three months old. In the death of husband and father a deep shadow was cast over the lonely widow and her six children, bereft of him who stood between them and a strange world. Robert Carmichael died six months after his arrival in Philadelphia with his family.

Society Pages – don't overlook them! Remember, small-town newspapers in particular look for anything that might be even the littlest bit newsworthy and of interest to their readers. A visit from a relative from the old country (pick a country – Ireland, England, Scotland, Germany, etc.) to an individual who had immigrated years earlier the United States would be news indeed! Wedding and birth announcements are standard fare for society pages. How about a significant anniversary, like this one from the *Seattle (Washington) Times*, Christmas Day, 1970:

Sherles observing 65th anniversary

They grew up together as children in Germany, were married in Russia, imigrated to Canada and settled in America.

Now Mr. and Mrs. John Sherle are observing their 65th year of marriage at their home at 420 N. 125th St.

Born in Stuttgart, they moved with their families to a German colony along the Black Sea of Russia. Married in Odessa, Russia, in 1905, they immigrated to Canada three years later.

From Winnipeg, the Sherles moved to a farm in Montana in 1912 and came to Seattle in 1937. Sherle worked as a cobbler here until his retirement.

The couple has four sons, Edward, Seattle; Otto, Way-

Mr. and Mrs. John Sherle

auwega, Wis.; Walter Havre, Mont., and Ted Sherle, Spokane; five daughters, Mrs. S. Robinson, Mrs. Clara Korssjoen, Mrs. Edward Felton and Mrs. Louis LeCompte, all of Seattle, and Mrs. Ida Baker, Las Vegas, Nev. Sherle is 88 and his wife is 81.

If you had been searching for information about this couple, note the immigration information mentioned (immigrated to Canada in 1908, and to America in 1912) along with information about their ages (88 and 83), marriage date and place (around December 25, 1905 in Odessa, Russia), their birth places (Stuttgart, Germany), children (four sons and five daughters). There is enough information about their movements and years of those movements, that you might also be able to follow clues to find the birthplaces of their children too. And of course their daughters' married names are listed.

Finally, here's a little piece from the *Wheeling (West Virginia) Register* from June 18, 1875. While it sounds a bit like those weekly e-mails I receive seeking my assistance from a prince in Africa, trying to get his father's fortune out of the country, it still provides me with immigration information about a couple (John Lawrence and Mary Townley Lawrence) who came to America before it was America:

THE Lawrences who reside in the Northern portion of this county are said to be interested in a fortune of $500,000,000 which is held by the Bank of England in trust for the legal heirs of John Lawrence and Mary Townley who imigrated to this county about the year 1713.— *Cambridge Jeffersonian.*

So when the going gets tough and you can't seem to unearth (no pun intended) that stubborn ancestor of yours, turn to the newspapers and see if you can find something there that will prove to break your search wide open. Most newspaper archives have pretty decent indexes, so simply typing your ancestor's name in the search field may yield the information you are seeking.

Genealogy Societies

If your immigrant ancestors came to a portion of the country where many of their former countrymen and family members had already settled, you may very well find a genealogy society devoted specifically to that group of immigrants. Your Polish ancestors came to Chicago in the mid-1800s? Then try the Polish Genealogy Society of America (*www. pgsa.org*) to see what immigration records and information they have available. A short detour there while I was writing this section provided me the opportunity to explore a large number of Polish-based databases, including information on immigrants, naturalization papers, birth and death records, marriage records, etc.

Your Italian relatives settled in one of the boroughs of New York City? Then by all means check out the Italian Genealogical Group of New York City (*www.italiangen. org*). A quick visit to this fine website listed many websites, including one titled *Passenger Lists, 1820 to 1897.*

Seek out genealogy societies near where my ancestors lived, or that address the ethnicity of my ancestors.

Your Irish ancestors came to Boston in the mid-19th century? Then be sure and see what the Boston to Providence Genealogy Society (*www. iment.com/bos2prov*) has to offer.

Ethnic Societies

Somewhat akin to genealogy societies, Ethnic Societies are also a potential source of information for your immigrant ancestors. When immigrants came to America, they often clustered in groups with others like themselves, especially for their first few years here. They were among their own, with folks who had the same language, traditions, etc. Perhaps they were joining family members in a distant city of this new country. Living closely together like this allowed those who had arrived earlier to be a source of assistance to newcomers who were coming to this big land with new laws, requirements and societal concerns.

Many formed heritage groups through the years – The Hibernians, The Swedish Connection, The Italians, etc. Often these groups published newspapers, kept records and celebrated weddings and births and noted deaths together. Searching the Internet for information about these societies may yield information on your ancestors that isn't available any place else. This information may be what you are looking for, or may serve as a clue as to where to find the information you are seeking.

Family Histories

Often, family histories are written that contain a wealth of information about individuals in a family. During the late 19th and early 20th centuries, these were particularly popular. The advantage of this is the authors often had access to the individuals about whom they were writing. Therefore, much of the information received was first-hand knowledge of many of the subjects of the book. Remember, however, that much of the information you find in family histories is considered secondary source information. That's okay – because it will give you clues and direction for finding primary sources.

Along with the first-hand knowledge of vital statistics – birth, death and marriage records — also comes stories and anecdotes about family members. I have enjoyed reading those through the years in family histories I have about several of my ancestral lines. They add color to the family and help these ancestors of mine become more human.

I have a number of these books in my possession – books that were written on the Grahams, the Throckmortons, the Sellers and the McQuillans. One thing I have noticed about these books – they are often fraught with error! Several of the books I have were published in the 1920s, one in the 1960s and one in the 1970s – long before the Internet was available for research. So be cautious with family histories that you run across. Use them to help you pinpoint accurate and error-free information.

One advantage of these older books, I have found, is that in the 19th and early 20th centuries, Americans were not quite as mobile as a society as we are now. Many times, numerous generations of a family were raised and died within 25 or 50 miles of their birthplace. Not so now – people move all over this great nation, and many even go abroad.

> Family histories are great – but be cautious! Errors enter in. Use them for clues to find primary resources.

My family is a great example of that. I have six children (one wife). During the twelve years those children were coming to our family, we lived in four states – Idaho, Utah, New Jersey and Colorado. We had children born in each of those states. If we do not keep good family records, some genealogical descendant of mine is likely to have a devil of a time finding records about our family. Adding to the confusion is that my wife and I were born in different states – different from each other and different from the four listed above. So – eight people in our family and six states represented among the birth states. I have a son who married in another state – Hawaii, and another son who married in Washington state. And I do not believe we are an oddity in America from a movement perspective.

However, as I was saying: while family members did move from the family nest, many times families stayed in the same area for generations. Many of my Quillen / McQuillan ancestors and other relatives have lived for three hundred years within a couple hours' drive from where Teague McQuillan, the first of my ancestors to arrive in America, arrived. The family history written about his family includes copies of deeds, birth, death and marriage certificates – all of which were basically local to the compilers of our family history. That's good news.

The LDS Church has a significant collection of family histories in their Family History Library in Salt Lake City, Utah, and available at their local

(4,500 worldwide) Family History Centers. At last count, their collection included over 60,000 family histories.

Local Histories

In the 1800s, it was fashionable to write county and town histories, which often included the biographies of prominent and/or early citizens of the county. I tend to think that my ancestors were largely like me – pretty normal, with occasional flashes of brilliance. Despite this relative normality, I have been successful in finding interesting and genealogically enlightening articles about several ancestors that have advanced my research efforts. Consider this short blurb that appeared in a book entitled *Biographies of Old Schuyler County (Illinois) Settlers*, written in 1878:

WILLIAM DEAN

William Dean was born in county Dennygaul, Ireland, May 3d, 1825, and is a son of John Dean. He received his early education in the district schools of Ireland. At about the age of twenty-two he emigrated to America, landing in New York. From there he went to the western part of Pennsylvania, where he resided two years. He then moved to Schuyler county, Illinois, in the spring of 1850, where he engaged in farming. In March, 1857, he was married to Mrs. Maria Pain, daughter of George and Jane Humphreys; she was born July 10th, 1830. The fruits of their marriage is a family of four children, one of whom is now deceased. Mr. Dean is at present residing on his farm in Littleton township, enjoying good health.

Mr. Dean happened to be the neighbor of my fourth great grandfather in central Illinois. Although not really considered an immigration record, this short biography helped establish important information about this immigrant, William Dean: his father's name, his marriage and number of children (one of which had died by 1878 when this article was written), his wife and her parents. Dates and places are included. This secondary source of information might be fraught with errors (for example, knowing a bit about Ireland and the Irish accent, I'd be willing to bet good money that Dennygaul, Ireland, is in reality *Donegal,* Ireland!), but the information provided is invaluable and can narrow your areas and timeframes for searches as you look for original immigration and naturalization documents to support this information. Were Mr. Dean your ancestor, you can use this information to narrow your search for his naturalization papers, knowing that he immigrated to America in about 1847 (at the height of the Great Potato Famine – there's that history stuff again!) and came through the port of New York.

When I was in high school, I was told I had been nominated with several other students in my high school to be in *Who's Who in American High Schools.* I thought that was pretty awesome. When we learned that to be included, I needed to purchase a copy of the book, my parents dutifully forked over the money. The blurb on me was short and sweet – I hadn't accomplished much by the advanced age of 18 – but it was kind of fun to see my name in lights, so to speak.

And so it was with some of yours and my immigrant ancestors. Many of these local histories focused on the important people of the community – early settlers, doctors, lawyers, business people, politicians, military men, etc. But common folk could also get in the books by paying a small fee – like I did to be in Who's Who. So – don't overlook these histories as a source of immigration information.

Funeral Home Records
Many genealogists (myself included until recent years) are totally oblivious of funeral records. Either they don't think about them, or if they do, they discount them as having relatively sparse information, or information of little value. Wrong answer! I stumbled upon the value of these records several years ago, and now regularly include them when I am digging for information.

Consider below the information I found on several folks as I was doing research in the area of Virginia from where many of my ancestors hail:

James Edward Payne, b. 11/10/1895 in Palmyra, Va., father – John Payne, mother – Ida Smith, death date – 9/30/1968, death place – Charlottesville, Va, burial Carter Cemetery, Palmyra, Va., children – Clinton, John, Annette Wood, Bernice Jones. Brother – Charlie Payne, Sisters – Madeline Giles, Mamie Branson, Ethel Brown. **Georgiana Wright**, b. 3/15/1908 in Albemarle City, Va., father – Harry Jones, mother – Elnora Maupin, death date – 8/18/1971, death place – Charlottesville, Va, burial Lincoln Cemetery, Palmyra, Va., children – Nicholas Jones, Luther & Earl Wright, Sadie White, Willetta Sadler, Annie Mae Johnson, Mary Gillian, Betty Ann Washington, Sylvia Estes, sister – Isabella Williams, husband – Luther D. Wright.

As you can see, a lot of genealogically significant information is in these entries. Had either party been born in a foreign land, then their place of birth would have been noted, and you would have had a clue about their origins.

So – if you run across funeral home records, don't turn up your nose at them! Sometimes you'll find them online, while others may come from contacting the funeral homes in the areas you are researching, either by phone or e-mail.

Voter Registration Records

Like funeral home records, voter registration records are often overlooked as a source of information on immigrants. Many counties throughout the United States have these records online, and they stretch back many decades. Often, these voter registration records include information about the voter's name, age, residence and place of birth. If the voter was not born in the US, then often the record will state what town and country in which the individual was born – another clue for you to follow up on.

If the individual was foreign born, they often had to prove that they had become a citizen, so naturalization information is also included. More on that aspect of voter registration records is covered in the *Naturalization Records* section.

For now, know that if you're having a hard time locating information about one or more of your ancestors, don't forget to search for them in voter registration records.

> Voter registration records are often overlooked as a source of naturalization information. Check them out!

5. NATURALIZATION RECORDS

In Chapter 3, we talked about the US censuses that asked a number of immigration questions – the 1900 through 1940 censuses. Often, these censuses may be the first place you find your immigrant ancestors. Answers to the immigration questions on the census may provide clues that will assist you in putting together the puzzle pieces to help you locate more information about these families, especially their naturalization records.

Let's consider the information you might glean from these questions, and where to go with that information. Once again, here are the questions:

> Censuses may provide important clues that will help you find your immigrant ancestors' immigration and naturalization records.

1. Year of immigration to the United States (1900, 1910, 1920, 1930, 1940)
2. Is the person naturalized? (1900, 1910, 1920, 1930, 1940)
3. If naturalized, year of naturalization (1920)
4. Whether able to speak English, or, if not, give language spoken. (1910, 1930, 1940)

Before we address those questions, a clue in your search for immigration records may be found in an unlikely place — at the top of the census sheet:

STATE *Oklahoma*

COUNTY *Pawnee*

TOWNSHIP OR OTHER DIVISION OF COUNTY *Eagle Township*

NAME OF INSTITUTION

DEPARTMENT OF
THIRTEENTH CENSUS

Many times, immigrating individuals filed their first papers – their Declaration of Intent – shortly after arrival in the United States. Sometimes they were excited to get the process started. Also, they often lived and worked near their port of entry into the United States, staying with friends or family for the first few months (or years!) after their arrival. But then, by the time their five-year residency requirement elapsed, and prior to filing their second papers – their Petition for Citizenship – they moved. Sometimes the move was to another town or city in the state, but it may have also been a move to another state, sometimes many miles from their original port of entry. Finding the family in the census may give you an idea of where to begin looking for their naturalization papers.

Okay – back to the questions as an assist in searching for records:

Question #1 – Year of immigration to the United States
This question, which was asked on the first four censuses of the 20th century, is helpful because it puts an early boundary on your search for naturalization records. If your ancestor immigrated in 1923, then you needn't look any earlier than that for their Declaration of Intent. Their submission of those first papers may have been relatively immediate, or years may have transpired between their arrival and the submission of their Declaration of Intent. Either way, you can rest assured they did not file their first papers before arriving here!

Question #2. Is the person naturalized? (1900-1940 censuses)
The answer to this question will potentially keep you from running down many blind alleys, searching for naturalization papers that do not exist. As mentioned in Chapter 3, women did not need to file naturalization papers to become citizens – until 1922, they rode in on their husband's citizenship coattails, and minor children got a free pass, too, as long as their fathers had gone through the citizenship process and been awarded citizenship. Answers to this census question can save you a lot of searching – or possibly even launch your search. If the answer is "No" to this question, then you need not search for naturalization papers for this

person. If, however, the answer is "Yes" to the question, then you should roll up your sleeves and start looking for those papers! Note, however, that just because your ancestor hadn't been naturalized by the time of this census, they could still naturalize later. If you continue to run into dead ends for that ancestor, be open to that possibility.

Question #3. If naturalized, year of naturalization (1920)
Again, this is a great question to add to the census. (It's too bad it wasn't repeated in the 1930 census.) This will help you further narrow your search for the naturalization papers for this individual.

Question #4. Whether able to speak English, or, if not, give language spoken. (1910, 1930)
While seemingly innocuous, this question may give you a clue on your ancestor's origins. For many years, Europe has been a collection of countries where borders were often blurred. French-speaking people lived in Germany, German-speaking people lived in France, Polish-speaking people lived in Russia, etc. This may give you a clue as to where to search for vital records for your ancestors.

As mentioned in the opening chapters, naturalization records refer to those records immigrants completed to become US citizens. There are several we'll deal with over the next few pages:

1. Declaration of Intent – these were papers completed to indicate the immigrant's intention to become a US citizen. They were often completed immediately upon arrival in the United States, but were sometimes completed later. These are often called *first papers*. These papers also have a great deal of genealogical information in them.

2. Petition for Naturalization – these papers were completed by the immigrant as part of his or her formal request to become a US citizen. Generally speaking, these could not be completed until an immigrant had been in the US at least five years. Also called *second papers* or *final papers,* as well as *Petition for Citizenship*. These papers usually have a great deal of genealogical information in them, and may have been filed many miles from where the immigrant first entered the United States.

3. Oath of Allegiance – this is the document the immigrant signs as s/he becomes a US citizen, renouncing allegiance to any other foreign power, dignitary, king, etc. Very little information of a genealogical value is contained in Oaths of Allegiance, but there may be some clues that will lead you to other sources of information.

4. Certificate of Arrival – Beginning June 26, 1906, immigrants completed a certificate of arrival upon their arrival in the United States. The form they completed was given to a clerk at the port of entry. He then checked the ship's passenger list, and if the immigrant was found on the list, a formal certificate of arrival was sent to the naturalization court. It provided a sort of double check, protecting against those who were trying to cheat the system.

Prior to 1906, when the federal government standardized the various naturalization documents, many variations were out there. Some contained a little information, some were somewhat more expansive in the information they asked. Though several of the naturalization documents provide similar information, there are also important differences that make finding them important. Following is the information that can be found on each of these documents beginning in 1906:

Declaration of Intent
Note: This document was also known as *first papers*.

• Court and location of filing
• Name
• Age
• Occupation
• Personal description (race, complexion, height, weight, color of hair and eyes, distinctive marks)

- Place of birth
- Date of birth
- Current residence
- Place from which they emigrated
- Ship they arrived on
- City of last foreign residence
- Married / not married
- Spouse's name, birth place and residence
- Renunciation of allegiance and fidelity to another foreign government
- Port of arrival in the United States
- Date of arrival in the United States
- Statements that the immigrant isn't an anarchist, polygamist or believer in polygamy
- Statement of the immigrant's intention to become a citizen of the United States
- Date the Declaration was filed

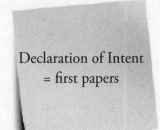

Declaration of Intent = first papers

The declaration of intent was valid for seven years.

Petition for Naturalization
Note: this form is sometimes called *Petition for Citizenship* and *second papers*.

- Court and location of filing
- Name
- Current residence
- Occupation
- Date of birth
- Place of birth
- Place from which they emigrated
- Date, place and court where they declared their intent to become a citizen of the United States
- Married / not married
- Spouse's name, birth date and birth place

Petition for Naturalization = Petition for Citizenship = second papers = final papers.

- Spouse's current residence
- Number of children, their names, dates and places of birth and current residence
- Renunciation of allegiance and fidelity to another foreign government
- Statement of the immigrant's intention to become a citizen of the United States
- That the immigrant is able to speak English
- Date since the immigrant has continuously lived in the United States
- A declaration that the immigrant has not filed for citizenship in the United States before
- The certificate number on the immigrant's declaration of intent
- The date of the immigrant's certificate of arrival
- The names and signatures of two witnesses who attest that they have known the person has lived continuously in the United States for at least five years
- The two witnesses attest to the good moral character of the immigrant
- The occupation and addresses of the two witnesses

Oath of Allegiance
- Name
- Date filed
- Renunciation of allegiance and fidelity to a foreign government
- If the immigrant wished to change his name, his former and his new name was identified
- Names and addresses of two witnesses

Certificate of Arrival
- Port of Entry
- Name of the immigrant
- Date of arrival
- Name of ship

The certificate of arrival was included with the petition for naturalization, unless the immigrant arrived before June 26, 1906.

As you can see, the first three of these documents are laden with genealogical information that is invaluable to a researcher. Even the certificate of arrival provides the name of the ship, date and port of entry for the immigrant. Armed with that information, a researcher can then seek the passenger lists for the ship, and perhaps learn much more about the immigrant.

Be sure you go beyond the obvious information contained in the naturalization documents. For example, check out the witnesses. Who are they? How did they know the immigrant? Could they have known him in the old country – were they neighbors? Relatives? As your research on a particular ancestor hits brick walls, backtrack and find out more about these witnesses who attested to the good moral character of your ancestor.

Let me reintroduce you to a family that was introduced to you earlier in the book, in the Immigration Records section. We had been exploring the Ellis Island website, searching for distant relatives of mine. We discovered this small family group, traveling without their husband / father:

• Elizabeth McQuillan, age 50
• James McQuillan, age 17
• Patrick McQuillan, age 15
• James McQuillan, age 9

We learned from the passenger list that Elizabeth also left her son William in Scotland when she departed for the United States. How difficult that must have been! As we learned from the second page of Elizabeth's passenger record, her husband's name is Adam McQuillan and he is living in Brooklyn, NY.

It's nice to know that Adam was alive and well, and living in Brooklyn, NY, but how do I find information about him? My natural inclination is to see if he had come to the United States through the same port of entry through which his family traveled. So I went to the Ellis Island website to see if I could find him. No such luck – no Adam McQuillan of sufficient age had come through Ellis Island. Rats.

But where to find Adam? If he didn't arrive in the United States through New York, then where? I decided to see if I could find a record of his arrival at one of the relatively nearby east coast cities – Baltimore, Philadelphia and Boston. I thought I would try Boston, since Boston was the port of entry for many Irish, and because more immigrants came through there than through Baltimore and Philadelphia. I went to Ancestry.com, where I knew there were Boston passenger lists online.

> Ancestry.com has many passenger lists online, including New York, Boston, Baltimore, Philadelphia, New Orleans and others.

Within minutes, I was rewarded – I found several Adam McQuillans who had arrived in the US through Boston. From the passenger list I found this Adam McQuillan.

The record told me that Adam was 53 years old, he was a machine man, was born in Ireland and his last residence was Clydebank, Scotland. He arrived at the port of Boston on the SS Haverford on September 5, 1923. The name of his nearest relative in Scotland was Elizabeth McQuillan, his wife. It looks like we found the right Adam McQuillan!

The second page of the passenger list provided more information about the McQuillan family. It tells us that Adam was born in Belfast, Ireland, and it said the relative he was going to join in the United Sates was Ellen McQuillan, his daughter, who lived at 75 3rd Avenue in Brooklyn, New York. So now, between Adam's and Elizabeth's Boston and New York passenger lists, we're beginning to get a picture of this Scottish / Irish family:

- Adam McQuillan, Head of Household, age 53
- Elizabeth McQuillan, Wife, age 50
- William McQuillan, son, age ? (Elizabeth's nearest relative in Scotland – listed as her son)
- Ellen McQuillan, daughter, age ? (the relative Adam was going to join in the US)
- John McQuillan, son, age 17
- Patrick McQuillan, son, age 15
- James McQuillan, son, age 9

Let me explain about one of the other Adams I found on the Boston passenger lists. I have done Irish research for many years, covering numerous family lines, and in my experience, Adam is not a common Irish name. Patrick, Daniel and Michael – yes. But not Adam. I noted that this second Adam was 27 years old, about the right age to be the son of a 53-year-old man. Also, he came from Clydebank, Scotland – the same town the elder Adam came from. The younger Adam listed Mary McQuillan of Clydebank, Scotland as his wife and nearest relative in his home country. The second page of the passenger list indicated that Adam was going to join his sister, Margaret McQuillan, who lived at 26 3rd Avenue in Brooklyn, New York.

I am surmising at this point that Adam the Younger belongs to Adam the Elder. I will keep his information and perhaps see if his family joins him later. But I am guessing that this Adam is the son of the elder Adam we have been discussing. This family is beginning to take shape!

It appears that Adam came to America about two months' ahead of his wife, John, Patrick and James. Ellen was already in America. Adam arrived on September 5, 1923 and Elizabeth arrived on November 3, 1923. Enough time for Adam to travel from Boston to Brooklyn, secure employment and a place to live for his family.

There is an interesting item on Adam's passenger list that will bear further exploration: When Adam said he was going to join his daughter Ellen McQuillan, he listed her information as:

Daughter: Ellen McQuillan
c/o Lundie 75 3rd Avenue, Brooklyn, NY

Often, immigrant husbands came to America ahead of their families, finding employment, securing a place to live, etc. Their families followed months or even years later.

It will be interesting to find out if Lundie is her married name, or perhaps friends she is living with. It might even be a family she is living with if she is a servant (a common thing in early 20th century – the Irish maid or Irish nanny). Or perhaps – it is a married sister. So many options! Something to look into later.

Also – is Adam the Younger's sister Margaret of 26 3rd Avenue in Brooklyn the same as Adam the Elder's daughter Ellen, who lives at 75 3rd Avenue in Brooklyn, or are these sisters, and Margaret is another daughter of Adam's and Ellen another sister of Adam's? Get your detective shoes on for this one! Back to our search for naturalization records. The information provided through these passenger lists is exciting, but it is just the beginning of our search. I must now take information gleaned from the passenger lists to find naturalization papers for these family members.

As you begin your search, remember two things:

1 A Petition for Citizenship could not be filed until five years after arrival in the United States. Therefore, the earliest Adam could apply would be September 1928, and

2. Women did not have to file naturalization papers. They could if they wished, but most preferred to become citizens by virtue of their husband's citizenship. Likewise, minor children did not need to petition for citizenship, they could also gain citizenship through their father, should he become a citizen.

Given those facts, it is entirely possible that we will not find citizenship papers for Elizabeth, Patrick or James. Patrick was 15 years old and James was 9 years old at the time of their arrival. Five years from their arrival date would make Patrick 20 years old and James 14 – both still minors in 1928 America. If Adam waits longer than five years to petition for his citizenship, then there may well be a petition for citizenship for Patrick as well, if he wanted to become an American citizen. John, of course, would have to file on his own, as he would be 22 before his father could apply for citizenship.

Women and children often received their citizenship through their husband / father, so there may be no naturalization records for them.

Some of the information on the passenger lists will assist me in finding the naturalization papers for the McQuillan family. Most important is knowing what ports of entry were used by the family. Other information important to our search is the vessel in which the immigrant arrived. In addition to helping us find the naturalization papers for the McQuillans, this information will help us ensure that when we do find naturalization papers, we can ascertain with certainty these are the McQuillans we're looking for.

Here is the information from the passenger lists that will help us take the next steps down the naturalization path:

1. Adam arrived in America on the ship Haverford on September 5, 1923 through the port of Boston.

2. Elizabeth and her children arrived in America on the ship Leviathan on November 3, 1923, and they arrived in New York.

Armed with that information, I can begin searching for Adam's – and John's – naturalization papers. Many immigrants were excited to become citizens, and filed their declarations of intent almost immediately upon their arrival in the country. Others waited until they got to the place where they intended to settle. So Adam's declaration of intent may be found in Boston (where he landed) or in New York (his destination). Since he said he was going to join his daughter Ellen in Brooklyn, I decided to look in New York first, although I could have looked in Boston first as well. Another reason for going to New York is that as of this writing, Boston naturalization records are not all online.

To seek his naturalization papers, I went to Ancestry.com. I went to their *Citizenship and Naturalization* section, and entered Adam's name. Nothing. I tried refining my search with different approaches, but still no luck.

> Check for naturalization papers in the city where your ancestor arrived as well as where he settled!

Not to be defeated, I decided to try searching through Fold3.com instead of Ancestry.com. While both have outstanding collections, sometimes Ancestry's is better, and sometimes Fold3's is better. I transferred my request to Fold3, and was rewarded with success! The first hit I got was Adam McQuillan's declaration of intent, filed October 17, 1932.

This is what I have been looking for, what I have been hoping to find. Note the critical information I learn about Adam and his family:

- Adam was living at 296 Moffat Street, Brooklyn, NY at the time he filed his declaration of intent.

- Adam gives his age as 62 years old.
- Adam was born March 17 (St. Patrick's Day!), 1870.
- His birth place is Newtownards, Ireland.
- His wife is Elizabeth.
- They were married July 13, 1894 in Glasgow, Scotland.
- Elizabeth was born in Glasgow, Scotland on January 8, 1874.
- Elizabeth immigrated to the US on November 3, 1923 through the port of New York.
- John says he has three children:
    John, born November 25, 1906 in Scotland;
    Patrick, born July 18, 1908 in Scotland;
    James, born June 20, 1913 in Scotland.
- An interesting note here – Adam says he filed a declaration of intent previously on April 2, 1924 in Brooklyn, New York.
- Adam immigrated to the US on September 5, 1923 on the vessel Haverford, arriving in Boston.
- This declaration of intent was filed on October 17, 1932.

Wow! The amount of information here is astounding (remember, though, as astounding as it is, it is all secondary information)! I learn of his birth place – Newtownards, Ireland. Given his and Elizabeth's arrival dates, I can confirm that these are in fact the right McQuillans, along with John, Patrick and James.

But there are a few discrepancies that need to be checked out:

1. On his passenger list, Adam claimed he was born in Belfast, not Newtownards.

    a. I have been to and around Belfast (one of the other hats I wear is a travel guide writer for Ireland). Newtownards is a country town about 10 miles east of Belfast. Not quite a suburb, but as he gave his information to whoever was recording the passenger list, he probably felt it would be best just to say Belfast. Sort of like Centennial is to Denver, Wooster is Boston, Glendale to Los Angeles, etc.

2. Adam only lists three children – John, Patrick and James, but we know for certain he has others:

    a. William, listed on Elizabeth's passenger list as her son;

    b. Ellen, listed on Adam's passenger list as his daughter;

    c. And what about Adam, another child I suspect they have;

    d. Perhaps Adam only felt he had to list his unmarried children.

That might be an explanation, but it bears looking into.

3. John McQuillan was listed as being 17 on the passenger list in 1923. With a birthday in November, that means he would have turned 18 two months later, so his birthday must have been in 1905. But Adam gives John's birth date as 1906. Hmmm – Elizabeth (or John) probably gave the information for the passenger list – I am betting Mom was right. It will be interesting to see if I can discover records for John that identify his correct birth date.

4. I at first thought it odd that Adam mentions that he had previously filed a declaration of intent in April 1924 – about seven months after he arrived. I wondered why he would file another declaration of intent? Then I recalled that declarations of intent are only valid for 7 years. The date of this declaration of intent is October 17, 1932 – 8 1/2 years later. I will reason then that he didn't get around to applying for citizenship within the requisite seven years, and in order to apply for citizenship, he had to file another declaration of intent. So – it's nice to know I am not the only procrastinator in the family!

As a special bonus, the declaration even had a picture of my distant cousin!

With Adam's declaration of intent in hand, I thought I would search to see if Elizabeth may have filed a declaration of intent. If she did, it might clear up several of the questions I raised above. I checked Ancestry and Footnote, to no avail. No declaration of intent for Mrs. McQuillan. So I looked for their son John's declaration of intent, and was successful when I searched through Footnote. Here's what I found for him:

- John was living at 58 Moffat Street, Brooklyn, NY at the time he filed his declaration of intent.
- John gives his age as 22 years old.
- John was born November 29, 1905.
- His birth place is Glasgow, Scotland.
- He is not married.
- John immigrated to the US on November 3, 1923 through the port of New York.
- This declaration of intent was filed on June 21, 1929.

So a couple of thoughts about John's declaration of intent:

1. His birth year is 1905 – not 1906 as his father thought, and his day of birth is November 29, not November 25, as his father thought. His dad was close, but a little off (or maybe not – see #3 below).

2. He appears to live a couple of blocks from his father – he lives at 58 Moffat Street, and his father lives at 296 Moffat Street.

3. John lists his age as 22 at the time he filed his declaration – in June 1929. But if he was born in 1905, he should be 23, getting ready to turn 24, not 22 getting ready to turn 23. Hmmm – maybe his father was right on his birth year after all. A conundrum to solve!

Earlier in this chapter I mentioned that Patrick might be able to gain citizenship by virtue of his father's citizenship, if his father was granted citizenship before Patrick became 21 years' old. As shown, even though Adam filed an initial declaration of intent in 1924, he did not follow it up and apply for citizenship, so his declaration became invalid. He therefore re-applied in 1932. That means Patrick, who was 15 in 1923 (and born in 1908, according to his father), would have been 24 by the time his father filed his second declaration of intent. That means Patrick would have to have filed for himself. A quick search on Fold3. com turned into a longer search, and I was unable to find a declaration of intent for Patrick. Sometimes that happens!

Another important document to find for immigrants is the certificate of arrival. As noted at the beginning of this chapter, the certificate of arrival does not list much that is genealogically critical. However, it does establish the city of entry into the United States, the date of that entry, and the ship upon which the immigrant traveled. This information can be found in a similar manner to the declarations of intent we mentioned above – checking online records, or getting microfilmed records through the LDS Church (they can be ordered and sent to a local Family History Center) or through NARA if you are fortunate enough to live near one of their regional facilities. Below is the certificate of arrival for Adam McQuillan, showing his port and date of entry, as well as the ship in which he traveled:

All this confirms the information we found on Adam's passenger list and declaration of intent.

Now that I have his declaration of intent and certificate of arrival, let's see if I can find his Petition for Citizenship (also called Petition for Naturalization). Since I have had success on Footnote in finding other paperwork for Adam, I try there first. My search is rewarded with Adam's Petition for Citizenship:

It is important to check the data on this document and make sure it coincides with the other data we have discovered from other sources. Significant differences might mean that this isn't the same Adam McQuillan.

Here's the genealogical information we glean from this document:

1. Adam was living at 296 Moffat Street, Brooklyn, NY – the same address he gave when he filed his declaration of intent.

2. Adam was born March 17, 1870.

3. His birth place is Newtownards, Ireland (this is important – we now have two records where he states that he was born in Newtownards, Ireland, and one where he says he was born in Belfast).

4. On his petition for citizenship, he says he filed his declaration of intent on October 17, 1932 – the exact date his declaration of intent carries.

5. His wife is Elizabeth.

6. They were married July 13, 1894 in Glasgow, Scotland – so that date is the same as Adam listed on his declaration of intent.

7. Adam says Elizabeth was born in Tlasgow, Scotland on January 8, 1872. Uh oh – a discrepancy here. I am going to assume Tlasgow is the same as Glasgow, but on this form he says Elizabeth was born in 1872, and on his declaration of intent he says she was born in 1874. Elizabeth gives her age as 50 on the passenger list in October 1923… which means her actual birth year would have been 1873. Hmmm – if we average the years Adam gave, we get 1873. A problem we'll have to solve through other records! But we're close.

8. Elizabeth immigrated to the US on November 3, 1923 through the port of New York – that checks out with all we know about her immigration trip from Scotland.

9. Adam says he has two children, John and Patrick:
   a. John, born November 25, 1906 in Scotland
   b. Patrick, born July 18, 1908 in Scotland

But what happened to James?! On his declaration of intent, James was listed as one of his children who was born on June 20, 1913. That would make him 22 at the time of Adam's petition for citizenship. Had he died? Or as we surmised earlier, did Adam not include his married children when asked to list his children? More problems to solve, more mysteries to unravel!

10. Adam immigrated to the US on September 5, 1923 on the vessel Haverford, arriving in Boston – which agrees with other information we have for him.

11. This petition for citizenship was filed on June 5, 1935.

So – while we are able to corroborate much of the information Adam gave earlier, we still have a few conundrums to noodle through, including:

— Was he really born in Newtownards instead of Belfast?
— What is Elizabeth's birth year?
— What happened to James? Was he dead at the time of Adam's petition for citizenship? Married? This is a mystery that still bears research.
— What about Adam the younger, Margaret and Ellen? These are other potential children of this family.

Remember – immigration and naturalization papers are considered secondary sources of information. For Adam, we were fortunate to find a number of immigration and naturalization papers, but as good as these are, as tremendous as the information is, we still have a number of discrepancies that will send us to other documents and sources to try and pinpoint exact dates and answer some of the questions that have been raised through these various sources.

> Immigration and naturalization records are generally secondary sources of information!

However, all that aside, we have discovered a great deal of information about these shirt-tail relatives of mine in a relatively short period of time. It has been worth my time and energy to seek out these records and to try and put the pieces of this family puzzle together.

Visa Applications

The immigration laws have changed through the years – in fact, some 150 changes have been made since the original Immigration Act of 1790. Many changes were minor, but others were more significant. One of the significant changes occurred in 1924. Legislation passed in mid-1924 required all immigrants to the United States to have a visa to enter.

The Immigration Act of 1924 went into effect on July 1, 1924. It required all those wishing to immigrate to the United States to apply for a visa. These visas could be procured at a US Embassy or consulate in the immigrant's home country. If approved, the visas were issued prior to the immigrant departing for the United States, and they were used for identification purposes once the immigrant arrived.

When immigrants arrived in the United States, immigration officials collected their visas. For those who were not immigrating, the visas were kept briefly at the port of entry of the individual, then later destroyed (what a loss!). For immigrants wishing to establish residency in the United States, their visas were collected and sent to Washington DC, where they were given a Visa File Number, and indexed by name, date and place of birth. This process was in place between July 1, 1924 and April 1, 1944.

On April 1, 1944, a new filing system was created. The Visa File Numbers were closed and stored, and new visas were place in files called A Files. The Visa File Numbered visas were put into 7,000 boxes and stored. Over three million pieces of paper are contained in those file boxes!

Visas were required for all immigrants beginning July 1, 1924

If you are searching for an immigrant ancestor among visa records, if you do not find them in the Visa File Numbers (for immigrants who arrived between July 1, 1924 and March 30, 1944), do not despair. For a variety of reasons, visa files may have been reopened; if that was the case for your ancestor, their file may have been renumbered and stored in the A files, or possibly in the C files (consolidated files). Persistence may be required!

I have been only able to find a few visas online – at the time of this writing, most are available only through the United States Citizenship and Immigration Services (USCIS) department of the federal government. One can only hope that these documents become part of a cooperative effort between the federal government and the likes of Fold3.com, Ancestry.com, etc. I am hoping that will happen soon. (More on the USCIS later.)

Visa files – especially if made more easily accessible – will be a boon for any researcher who has immigrant ancestors who entered the country after 1924. The application has the following information:

— applicant's full name;
— date of birth;
— place of birth;
— names of the immigrant's parents;
— all the immigrant's addresses for the five years previous to their emigration – great clues to follow up on!

But wait – it gets better! All the visa applications after July 1, 1924 required a certified copy of a birth certificate. Many visa applications included marriage certificates, military service records, affidavits of support and various types of correspondence. If the immigrant had no birth certificate, an affidavit was required explaining the absence of official or church records, and the signature of a person who could aver that the birth information that was provided was true. That person had to be in a position to personally know the information – so it was often a relative – mother, father, grandparent, aunt, uncle, etc. More clues!

Immigration and Naturalization Service. I mentioned this organization a few paragraphs earlier. This is a department of the federal government. The name is now the United States Citizenship and Immigration Services (US-CIS) (catchy, don't you think!?). Their website is *www.uscis.gov*. If you go to that site, from the home page, look at the bottom right-hand side, under *Other Services*, and click on *History* and *Genealogy*, and from that page, click *Genealogy*. This is where you can find the records you're after.

INS = USCIS

The USCIS (it's too long to spell out more than once!) has a copy of all naturalization records kept from 1906 to 1956. Before you get too excited, it is very expensive to get records from the USCIS – they charge $20 to search their files to see if they have information on an ancestor you can identify discretely enough for them to find a match in their records. If they find a possible match, you will be notified (and charged $20). They will also provide you with the file number (called a citation number), instructions on how to order the file, and the form you must use to order it.

If you then decide to order the file and follow the instructions properly, you may get the files for a fee that ranges between $20 and $35, depending on the type of file located and provided. (Microfilmed records cost $20 and hard copy records cost $35.) So, the cost for the file, including the index search fee, ranges between $40 and $55. (They seem to be chipping away at the multi-trillion national dollar debt, one immigrant ancestor at a time!)

The USCIS website warns numerous places that you need to ask for files using a specific citation (file) number. Not to do so may result in receipt of the wrong information, or may return a result of "No Records." Either way, you pay the fee. So make sure you get the appropriate citation number!

One of the notes on the USCIS website says:

> **Important**: A single immigrant may have several USCIS records. For example, an immigrant who entered the US in 1924 and naturalized in 1930 may have both a Visa File and a C-File. An index search returns citations for *all* of an immigrant's records, while a Records Request without Case ID will return only the specific file(s) requested. Researchers who wish to know about all of an immigrant's USCIS records should file an Index Search request.

Following are the kinds of records available through the USCIS:
• **Certificate Files (C-files)** from 27 September 1906 to 1 April 1956
• **Alien Registration Forms** from 1 August 1940 to 31 March 1944
• **Visa Files** from 1 July 1924 to 31 March 1944
• **Registry Files** from 2 March 1929 to 31 March 1944
• **Alien Files (A-files)** numbered below 8 million (A8000000) and documents therein dated prior to May 1, 1951

As you request information for your immigrant ancestor, you'll need to provide the correct citation (file) number, their full name, birth date (actual or estimated), and their country of birth. If their birth date is within the last 100 years, you'll also need to provide proof they have died.

When working with the USCIS, be sure and get the right citation number for files!

Below is further information on each type of record held by the USCIS. It is taken directly from their website:

Certificate Files

Certificate Files, or C-files as they are called, are a product of the Basic Naturalization Act of 1906, which created the Federal Naturalization Service and required the new agency to collect and maintain duplicate copies of all court naturalization records. Initially, courts forwarded copies of Declarations of Intention, Petitions for Naturalization, and naturalization certificates to Washington,

D.C. Later, Congress expanded the Naturalization Service authority to create additional C-Files relating to derivative and resumed U.S. citizenship, as well as repatriation.

C-Files dated 1906 to ca. 1944 (C-1 to C-6500000) were microfilmed in the 1950's. Sadly, the original files were destroyed. The only C-files below C-6500000 remaining in paper form are those that were 1) unavailable at the time of filming or 2) re-opened after microfilming for further action. Immigrants with C-Files below C-6500000 may have additional USCIS files depending on their arrival date or naturalization date. Some C-Files below C-6500000 are Consolidated C-Files and are the only file for that individual.

C-Files C-6500000 to approximately C-7700000 (to 31 March 1956) are considered "Consolidated C-Files" containing all agency records on that individual subject.

Since 1906 standard naturalization forms called for the immigrant's name, date and place of birth, and port and date of arrival. When applicants claimed arrival after 30 June 1906, the Naturalization Service verified the arrival information by checking the original immigration record.

Despite the standardization mandated by the 1906 naturalization law, standard C-Files do vary by date and the circumstances of the naturalization. The content of a C-file usually depends upon when the person naturalized, under what provisions of law they applied, and whether or not there was any further activity in their case after naturalization. Many naturalization cases re-opened later in connection with applications for replacement (or lost) certificates, derivative citizenship claims, requests for proof of citizenship in relation to job applications, background investigations, insurance claims, or pension benefits.

C-Files also include several certificate series not duplicated in court records, such as derivative citizenship certificates (A series, AA series), and certain repatriation and resumption of citizenship files. There are ten types of C-Files.

Alien Registration Files

Alien Registration files (as opposed to enemy alien registration) began in August 1940 as a program intended to fingerprint and create a record of every non-citizen within the United States. The original Alien Registration Act of 1940 was a national security measure, and directed the Service to fingerprint and register every alien age 14 and older living within and entering the United States. The 1940 Act directed that a specific form be developed for the Alien Registration program. INS then introduced the Alien Registration Form (AR-2), a form individually stamped with a unique Alien Registration Number. Forms AR-2 date from August 1, 1940 to March 31, 1944.

Alien Registration Forms completed between August 1940 and March 1944 were microfilmed and the original forms were destroyed. USCIS maintains this microfilm containing 5,665,983 Alien Registration Forms (AR-2). The microfilmed forms are technically not part of the A-File series. Alien Registration Forms available from this series include files on:

• Resident aliens and delayed registrations, August 1940 through March 1944
• Railroad workers, 1942 through 1943
• Children under 14 years of age, resident in the US, August 1940 through March 1944
• Newly arriving immigrants (consular registrations) August 1940 through March 1944. Alien Registration forms on microfilm are arranged in numerical order, and are indexed by name, date of birth, and place of birth.

Though not official arrival records, Alien Registration Forms dating from the early 1940s may be useful in documenting an individual's presence in the United States. Many resident aliens registered under the Alien

Registration Act during 1940-1941 had been living in the United States for decades. Some arrived as early as the 1880s and the Alien Registration form is the agency's only record of that immigrant.

The registration form (Form AR-2) asked for the information listed below. Remember that not all registrants provided all information.

- Name
- Name at time of entry to the US
- Other names used
- Address
- Date of Birth
- Citizenship/Nationality
- Gender
- Marital Status
- Race
- Height & Weight
- Hair & Eye Color
- Port, date, ship and class of admission at last arrival in US
- Date of first arrival in US
- Years lived in US
- Intended stay in US
- Usual occupation
- Present occupation
- Present employer, including address
- Club, organization, or society memberships
- Military service (country, branch, dates)
- Date and number of Declaration of Intent (if filed), and city and state where filed.
- Date of Petition for Naturalization (if filed), and city and state where filed.
- Arrest history
- Fingerprint
- Signature
- Date and place of registration

Visa Files

July 1, 1924, was the effective date of the Immigration Act of 1924. That law required all arriving immigrants to present a visa when applying for admission. Immigrants applied for the visas at U.S. Embassies and Consulates abroad, and the State Department issued visa documents to approved immigrants before they departed for the United States.

Upon arrival, Immigrant Inspectors at the ports of entry collected "visa packets" from arriving immigrants and filed them in one of two ways: NON-Immigrant visas were filed temporarily at the ports of entry and were later destroyed. Immigrant (i.e., permanent admission) visas were sent to the Central Office in Washington for filing. At the Central Office, the visas were arranged by date and port of arrival, stamped with a unique Visa File number (see Record Request Issues, below), and indexed by name, date of birth, and place of birth. Beginning April 1, 1944, all new visas were filed in A-Files and the Visa Files series closed.

Between July 1, 1924 and March 31, 1944, Visa Files were the official arrival records of immigrants admitted for permanent residence. As such, they were used on a daily basis for verification of arrival for naturalization and other purposes. Passenger lists and border port manifests remained the official record of non-immigrant admissions in those years.

The Visa Files series was retired to storage in 1952, and consists of more than 3.1 million paper files filling nearly 7,000 boxes. The agency routinely retrieves Visa Files from storage in response to applications for naturalization or other benefits, Freedom of Information Act requests, and Genealogy requests.

Researchers should note that if an immigrant's case re-opened after April 1, 1944, the Visa File may have been removed from the series and placed inside an A-File or a C-File (files consolidation). If the consolidation occurred between 1944 and 1975, the index will only refer to the A-File or C-File.

If the consolidation took place since 1975 the Genealogy Program will perform additional steps to identify the file containing the visa packet.

Visa Files are among the most valuable immigration records for genealogical research. The application form itself contains the immigrant's complete name, date of birth, and place of birth, as well as the names of his/her parents. Also on the form will be the immigrant's address(es) for the five-year period prior to emigration.

Of most value to many researchers is the photograph on the front of the visa packet. Attached to the visa application are vital records required by the Immigration Act of 1924. In most cases these include a certified copy of a birth certificate, health certificate, and police or "moral" certificate (the results of a record check done by the authorities in the old country). Some visas include marriage certificates, military service records, affidavits of support, or correspondence. When the birth record is absent there is usually an affidavit explaining the absence of official or church records and offering the testimony of an individual in a position to know the circumstances of the immigrant's birth.

Registry Files
Registry Files document the creation of official immigrant arrival records under the Registry Act of March 2, 1929, which applied to persons who entered the United States prior to July 1, 1924, and for whom no arrival record could later be found.

The Basic Naturalization Act of 1906 first required a record of lawful entry/admission as a prerequisite to naturalization. The effect of the new law became apparent five years later, in 1911, when numerous immigrants were unable to naturalize because there was no record of their admission, or no such record could be found. These people could not naturalize until Congress provided relief with the Registry Act of 1929.

Registry Files document the first "legalization program" authorized by

Congress. The law and program allowed immigrants subject to the Certificate of Arrival requirement for naturalization, but for whom no arrival record could be found, to have a record of their original arrival created. Though dating after 1929 the records actually relate to immigrant

USCIS = $$$, so exhaust all other sources

arrivals occurring many years before. Registry Files from 1929 to 1944 generally relate to immigrant arrivals between June 29, 1906 and July 1, 1924. The initial Registry program applied to immigrants who arrived before July 1, 1921. Later, as time passed, Congress moved the ending date progressively forward.

Registry Files survive in their original paper form. They contain applications, testimony, evidence, correspondence, a photo, and a decision granting or denying Registry. They are arranged by Registry File Number (i.e., R-#####) and indexed by name and number.

Registry Files are treasures for the few genealogists whose immigrant ancestors who applied (there are only about 1/4 million Registry Files). The Registry application is full of dates, places, and names, an account of the immigrant's travel to the United States as well as accounting for their activities (employment, residence) since arrival. In addition to the application the files typically hold correspondence, affidavits, testimony, and other related papers. Documentary evidence can include school records, insurance receipts, rental agreements, or anything establishing the immigrant's residence prior to July 1, 1924.

As you can see, and as we have discussed throughout this book, these records held by the USCIS could contain genealogical information of inestimable value to genealogical researchers. However, it is complex, time-consuming and expensive to have the USCIS do the research for you. One search would pay for a three-month subscription to Ancestry. com, and two searches would pay for three-month subscriptions to Ancestry.com *and* Fold3.com, two of the best subscription services available to genealogists.

Because of the cost of these searches, I suggest you exhaust all other efforts to find the records for your immigrant ancestors prior to paying the fees charged by the USCIS. Also note the dates of the records held by the USCIS date to when the federal government took over the immigration and naturalization processes – 1906. Immigrant ancestors who came prior to 1906 will not be contained in their files.

Another possibility is to see if some of these records you are searching for are located at one of NARA's regional facilities. Sometimes, those records are available for you to see and copy for no cost. Often, the website for the regional facility nearest you may have information about their immigration and naturalization holdings. For example, the website for the Denver Regional NARA facility has this little blurb:

Our microfilm holdings are:
- **Of genealogical interest** – Federal population censuses for all States, 1790-1930; some pre-1900 military service and pension records, and bounty land warrant applications; selected passenger arrival records and indexes for vessels arriving at various U.S. ports; some naturalization papers and indexes for Colorado, Montana, and New Mexico, and some Indian censuses for Colorado, Montana, New Mexico, South Dakota, Utah, and Wyoming.

If I had immigrant ancestors who settled in Colorado, Montana or New Mexico, some of their naturalization records might be available right here in my own back yard! And at much lower cost than if I ordered them from the USCIS.

Genealogy Societies
Wait a minute – you may have noted that earlier in this book I mentioned that Genealogy Societies were sources of immigration records. While that

is true, I have also listed them here as a source of naturalization records, because these are records that genealogy societies are active in finding and reproducing. In the *Immigration Records* section, I suggested that if your ancestors were Italian and had settled in the New York City area, you should check out the Italian Genealogical Group of New York City (*www.italiangen.org*). In addition to the database for Passenger Lists I found there, I also found the following databases devoted to naturalization records:

- Eastern District Naturalizations, 1865 – 1957
- Southern District Naturalizations, 1824 – 1959
- Nassau County Supreme Court District Naturalizations, 1899 – 1989
- Suffolk County Naturalizations, 1865 – 1981
- Bronx Borough Supreme Court Naturalizations, 1914 – 1952
- Queens Borough Supreme Court Naturalizations, 1906 – 1957
- Clinton County Naturalizations, 1965 – 1906
- Essex County Naturalizations, 1836 – 1906
- Northern County Naturalizations
- Richmond Naturalizations
- Camden, NJ Naturalizations Index
- Trenton, NJ Naturalizations Index
- Alien Statements
- Western District Naturalizations
- Military Naturalizations

Wow – what a great find. A trip to one of the databases allowed me to enter a surname, after which I received the following information:

- Immigrant's first and last name
- Age
- Petition number
- date of petition
- approximate year of birth
- Soundex code for the name

This is the website of one of thousands of genealogy societies in the United States devoted to finding the records of immigrant ancestors. To find those who may be preserving and making available the records for your immigrant ancestors, simply Google to look for them: Polish Genealogy Society, Swedish Genealogy Society, Irish Genealogy Society, etc. I think you'll be pleasantly surprised with what you find. You may narrow your search by adding the state or city you are most interested in.

Don't reinvent the wheel: genealogy societies may have already unearthed information about your immigrant ancestors!

If your immigrant ancestors came to a portion of the country where many of their former countrymen and family members had already settled, you may very well find a genealogy society devoted specifically to that group of immigrants. Your Polish ancestors came to Chicago in the mid-1800s? Then try the *Polish Genealogy Society of America* (*www.pgsa. org*) to see what immigration records and information they have available. A short detour there while I was writing this section provided me the opportunity to explore a large number of Polish-based databases, including information on immigrants, naturalization papers, birth and death records, marriage records, etc.

Your Swedish ancestors settled in the chilly state of Minnesota? Then by all means check out the *Swedish Genealogical Society of Minnesota* (*www.sgsmn. org*). A quick visit to their fine website listed many resources for Swedish research, for records in both Minnesota and Sweden.

Voter Registration Records
Do not pass right over voter registration records! You might suppose that a voter registration record certainly wouldn't provide any genealogical data, much less data about an immigrant ancestor's naturalization. If you thought that, you might very well be wrong. Some voter registration records contain the bare minimum information. But others provide clues that can be very valuable in finding more information about your ancestors.

Take for example the Chicago (Cook County) Illinois voter registration record for 1892. Following are a couple of pages from that voter registration list:

Note the information I can glean on these individuals: their address, land of nativity, length of time they have lived in the precinct, county and state, and whether they are native Americans or have been naturalized.

Following is the second page of this voter registration record for these men:

Note that the first four men from page 1 were foreign born – two in Ireland and two in Scotland. We can see from the far-right column of page 1 that they have been naturalized; on page 2, we learn the date of their naturalization papers, and the court where they filed their papers – huge clues to assist us in tracking down their papers. Alexander McQuatter, formerly of Scotland (the fourth voter on the page) filed his papers in 1856 in the County Court of Poughkeepsie, NY – a long way from Chicago, Illinois. Without this clue, Mr. McQuatter's family may have searched and searched without successfully finding his naturalization papers.

I recently viewed the transcription of voter registrations for Orleans Parish Louisiana (New Orleans). Information contained there would have been very valuable had I an immigrant ancestor living (and voting!) in that area. By scanning its contents, I would be able to glean information about individuals that would be helpful in my search for specific naturalization records: their country of birth as well as when and where they were naturalized – great clues that would assist me in finding the naturalization papers for these individuals. As in the example from Cook County, Illinois, there was an immigrant living in New Orleans whose naturalization papers were filed in the City Court of Yonkers, NY. Without this information, I might have spun my wheels for years trying to locate this ancestor's naturalization papers in and around New Orleans – especially since New Orleans was a port through which immigrants passed. And if his naturalization papers were filed in Yonkers, it's a good bet he arrived in the United States through a New York – or at least northeastern — port, and not New Orleans!

During my review of those records, I also noted that many of these individuals registered to vote on the same date they were naturalized – a red letter day in their lives! There were also numerous individuals in the register with the same surname and same country of origin – certainly worth checking out to see if there were any familial relationships among them.

Don't overlook voter registration records as a possible source of more information about your immigrant ancestors!

6. OTHER RECORDS

In addition to the records that are specifically designed to collect information about our immigrant ancestors (passenger lists, naturalization petitions, declarations of intent, etc.), there are a number of other records that can be used to glean information about immigrant ancestors.

Death certificates

A number of death certificates I have reviewed over the years have included information about immigration. Consider the death certificate for this distant cousin:

> Death certificates may provide clues to finding naturalization records!

Note the question near the top of the certificate (indicated by the arrow) that asks how long the individual had been in the United States, if they were foreign born. As you can see, Patrick McQuillan, who died at the age of 73 in 1924, had been in the United States for the past 38 years. So – my search for immigration and naturalization records has a timeframe we can focus on – approximately 1886 is the year Patrick immigrated to the United States. Note the other genealogical information provided by this immigrant's death certificate: the name of his father and his mother's maiden name, and that he as well as they were born in Ireland. It is a shame that the town in Ireland where Patrick was born is obscured; it almost looks like St. Patrick. Hmmm – wonder how many places in Ireland have that name! Note also that the person providing the death information is *Sister Benedict* – probably a nun, which might also give us a clue as to Patrick's religion.

Below is another certificate that may have provided a clue, had this person been foreign born:

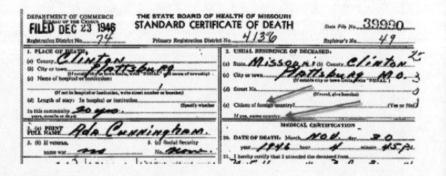

Alien Enemy Registration records

I am sure you are aware that not everyone who immigrated to America became a citizen. When World War I and then again when World War II broke out, because of concerns about non-citizen immigrants (aliens) living within the borders of our country, all such individuals were required to register with the government. These registration periods ran from November 1917 to April 1918, then again between August 1, 1940 and March 31, 1944. All aliens age 14 and over were required to register and have their fingerprints placed on file. The following questions were asked of aliens:

World War I:
• Full name (including maiden name for females)
• Current residence and length of residence
• Place of birth
• Spouse's name and residence
• Children's names, sex, and years of birth
• Parents' names (including maiden name for mother), birthdates, and birth places
• Names, dates of birth, and current residence of siblings
• Whether any male relatives were serving in the military for/against US
• Whether the alien had registered for selective draft
• Previous military or government service
• Date of immigration, name of vessel and port of arrival
• Whether naturalized in another country
• Whether reported/registered with a consul since 1 June 1914
• Whether applied for naturalization or took out first papers; if yes, when and where
• Whether ever taken an oath of allegiance other than to the United States
• Whether ever arrested or detained on any charge
• Whether held a permit to enter a forbidden area

A full description, photograph and set of fingerprints were also included. Wow – great information to find on an immigrant ancestor. Following is the digital image of two of the pages of one such registration form from the World War I registration period:

UNITED STATES OF AMERICA

Department of Justice

REGISTRATION AFFIDAVIT OF ALIEN ENEMY

The registration affidavit must be filed in and sworn to in triplicate and accompanied by four unmounted photographs of the registrant, not larger than 3 by 3 inches in size, on thin paper with light background. All four photographs should be signed by registrant across the face of the photograph so as not to obscure the face, if registrant is able to write. If registrant is unable to write, he must make his mark in the signature space and affix his left thumb print in the space indicated for the same opposite the signature.

The affidavit need not be filed out before, but must be signed and sworn to before, a registration officer, who will fill in the description and take the finger prints of the registrant. All registration officers are authorized to administer the oath hereon to persons registering as alien enemies.

I, _Max Amelang_ hereby register as an alien enemy

at _Kingman, Arizona_ and make the following statements

and answers under oath:

1. Name _Max Amelang_ All other names at any time used _____
   No need to use any other name

2. Present residence _Kingman, Arizona_

3. Length of residence at the foregoing place _October 1916_

4. All other places of residence since January 1, 1914 _Albia, Iowa, Ottumwa, Ia.,_

5. Born in _Cothen Anhalt_ on _10-30-1890_

6. Since January 1, 1914, employed by:

Name of place	Date	Occupation	Name of employer
Albia, Iowa	6-1-14/1-31-15	Bookkeeper	Acme Telephone Co
Ottumwa, Iowa	2-1-15/5-27-16	"	John Morrell & Co
Moline, Ills	5-9-16-7/16	"	Moline Plow Co
Went to the west			
Kingman, Az	10/15-16	"	J. M. George

7. I entered the United States _April 25 1914_ at the port of _New York_

   on ship _Kaiser Wilhelm II_ and applied for entry under the name of _Max Amelang_

8. (a) Name of father _Vincent Amelang_ Living _Yes_

   Residence of father, if living _Cothen - Anhalt, Germany_

   (b) Name of mother _Henriette Amelang_ living _Yes_

   Residence of mother, if living _Cothen Anhalt Germany_

2

9. State particulars of family as follows:

a. Married? *No* (Answer "Yes" or "No.") Name of wife _____ Wife living? _____ (Answer "Yes" or "No.")

Residence of wife, if living _____

b. Names of children between 10 and 14 years of age in the United States:

Names.	Sex.	Year of birth.

None

c. Number of children under 10 years of age _____

d. State whether registrant has or has had any male relatives in arms for or against the United States and its allies during the present war. *Yes* (Answer "Yes" or "No.") If "yes," give particulars:

Names.	Relationship.	For or against.
Otto Amelang	Cousin	For
Alfred Amelang	Brother	Against
Carl Amelang	Brother	Against
Albert Schumacher	Brother-in-law	Against
2 Cousins		

10. Were you registered for the selective draft? *Yes* (Answer "Yes" or "No.") Where? *Kingman City* (State district of registration.)

11. State all previous military or naval or other Government service. *none* (Here state duties, direction, and character of military or naval or other service and nation for which registrant served.)

12. Have you ever applied for naturalization or taken out first papers of naturalization in the United States? *Yes* (Answer "Yes" or "No.") If yes, state when and where *March 15 1916 Altoona Pa* (Give State or Territory, city, town, or other municipality, and name of court.)

13. Have you ever been naturalized, partly or wholly, in any country other than the United States? *no* (Answer "Yes" or "No.") If yes, state when and where and in what country _____

14. Have you ever taken an oath of allegiance to any country, State, or nation other than the United States? *no* (Answer "Yes" or "No.") If yes, state when and where and to what country _____

4-7069

The important information we can glean from this record includes:

• his date of arrival in the United States
• the port of entry he used when he arrived
• the name of the ship on which he arrived
• his birth date
• his birth place
• his parents' names and their residence
• the names of brothers, a brother-in-law and a cousin who were involved in the war
• the fact that he had registered for the draft, and where (more information!)
• the date and place where he filed his naturalization (Ottumwa, Iowa – Radar O'Reilly would be proud!)

Had Mr. Amelang had children, information about them would also have been included on his Alien Enemy Registration form.

It also provided the residences he had while living in the United States, and the dates when he lived in those places. These are important clues that could help us find other information – birth records for children, where he might have lived during a particular census, etc.

Note: Since Max indicated he had registered for the draft in Kingman, AZ, I thought I would try to find his Draft Registration card. Within just a few minutes I located it on Ancestry.com. I was able to verify information like his birth place and date and when and where he applied for naturalization. I also discovered he was exempt from the draft because he was deaf in his right ear.

On the next page see his World War I Registration Card:

Some alien enemy registration forms were also accompanied by a photograph of the alien. As you can see, these records – especially those from 1917-1918 — provide invaluable genealogical information.

Below are several abstracted reports of alien registrations that took place in Minnesota during the World War I registration period:

MERKLEIN, BABBETTE
    m.n. Babbette Fox - b. Wutternburg, Germany, Dec. 27, 1868 -
h. Fredrick - ch. Minnie Lallow, b. Feb. 7, 1890; Fred, b. Oct. 4, 1891,
U.S. Army; Elizabeth, b. Oct. 24, 1893; Pauline, b. Apr. 1, 1899;
Carl, b. Oct 19, 1901; Clara, b. Dec. 20, 1904 (all residents of F.W.)
f. Michael Fox (dec.), b. Wittenberg, Germany - m. Barba (englehart)·
Fox (dec.) - bro. Henry, b. June 5, 1865, res. F.W.; Fred, b. Nov.,
1866, res. F.W. - sis. Minnie Neukom, b. June 29, 1875, res. F.W.
arr. Nov. 21, 1890, pt. N.Y., sh. Fulta·, u.n. Babbette Fox

MERTENS, CLARA
    m.n. Clara Kreckmann - b. F.W., Feb. 14, 1874 - ch. Myrtle, b. June
30, 1896; Helen (?), b. Nov. 18, 1898; Velma, b. Feb. 8, 1900; Herbert,
b. Oct. 13, 1902; Margaret, b. Mar. 29, 1907; Elenne, b. Feb. 26, 1909;
Ruth, b. Feb. 26, 1911; Donald, b. May 11, 1914; Willis, b. Dec. 18,
1916 (all residents of F.W.) - f. Michael Kreckmann, b. Germany, res.
F.W. - m. Louisa (Gephard) Kreckmann, b. New York, res. F.W. - bro.
Fred, b. Oct. 9, ----, res. F.W.; Charles, b. Jan. 24, ----, res. F.W.
sis. Anna Carey, b. Jan. 3, ----, res. Indianapolis, Ind.; Millie Pauley,
res. F.W.

Note the immense amount of genealogical information that can be
gleaned from these two alien registration abstracts. Birth (and in some
cases, death) dates and places, maiden names of the women, spouses,
children and their birth dates, brothers and sisters, etc. A great find.

World War II
Alien registration records from World War II are not yet available due
to privacy laws, but they soon will be. Following is the information
requested on the forms each alien was required to complete:

• Full name
• Name at time of entry to the US, if different than current
• Other names used
• Current address
• Date and place of birth
• Citizenship/Nationality
• Gender
• Marital status
• Race
• Height & Weight
• Hair & Eye Color

- Date, port, vessel and class of admission of last arrival in US
- Date of first arrival in US
- Number of years in the US
- Usual occupation
- Present occupation
- Name, address and business of present employer
- Membership in clubs, organizations or societies
- Dates and nature of military or naval service
- Whether citizenship papers were filed and if so the date, place, and court
- Number of relatives living in the US
- Arrest record, including date, place and disposition
- Whether or not affiliated with a foreign government

As you search for the forms, don't be surprised to run across the terms *Registration Affidavit of Alien Enemy* form and *Registration Affidavit of Alien Female* form – male non-citizens completed the former and female non-citizens completed the latter!

Passport Records
Why include passport records in a book about immigration and naturalization records? There are several answers.

First, many, perhaps most, immigrants left significant portions of their families behind as they headed for the Promised Land that was America. Aging (or not so aging) parents, grandparents, siblings, and children were left behind. As we researched the McQuillan family in earlier chapters of this book, remember that Elizabeth McQuillan's passenger list record indicated that her nearest relative in Scotland was her son, William, who lived in Clydebank, Scotland?

Second, I can't tell you how many passport applications I have reviewed that listed as a reason for the return to the immigrant's native land things like:

- returning to settle an estate

- returning to close out a business
- returning to sell my farm

And so on – in addition to family members to visit, lives were left behind and things still needed attending to.

And don't forget – their native homeland represented a tempting destination for those who were able to make their fortune (or at least a living) in America, and they wanted to return to the home country for a vacation and visit. For example, it is interesting to note that even today, it is estimated that 70% of American travelers to Ireland have Irish ancestors. I have made that pilgrimage, even though most of my ancestors, and especially my McQuillan ancestors, have been in America for several hundred years. There is just an irresistible draw to the home country for many. How much more so for those who themselves left that cherished homeland!?

> Immigrant ancestors traveled back to their native land for a variety of reasons.

As with so many of the other immigration and naturalization records we have discussed, the questions asked of those making application for a passport varied throughout the history of our country. Passports were not required until 1941; prior to that they were available and recommended, but not required (except for brief periods during the Civil War and World War I). Even at that, the National Archives has nearly two million passport applications on file for travelers between 1795 and 1925. The applications for these passports sometimes provide genealogical information.

Until the first quarter of the 20th century, the vast majority of passports (95%) were issued to men. This doesn't mean women didn't travel abroad; until the 1920s, women and children traveling with their husbands were listed on their husband's or father's passport.

Unlike today's passports that are good for ten years (for adults), passports in the early years of the United States were valid for two years; therefore, you may find numerous passports for your ancestors.

The information found on passport applications varied through the years, but at a minimum they usually listed at least the full name, birth date and birth place of the individual. Many provided the physical description, which though not particularly of genealogical value, provide an interesting glimpse of an ancestor whom you would otherwise have no way of knowing what he or she looked like. Consider, for example, the application of Mr. Philip F. McQuillan (see next page).

Mr. McQuillan's passport application provided the following information:

• he was born in Ireland (would have been nice to have a city named!)
• his birth date was March 11, 1834
• he made his application in 1874, when he was 40 years old
• his wife and a minor daughter were traveling with him, and the daughter is listed as being 7 years old
• his naturalization papers were filed in the Circuit Court of Davis County, Illinois on March 14, 1855
• and of course his description

I reviewed another application for a gentleman who was born in Ireland in 1870. It listed the above information, but also included the name of the applicant's father, the father's birthplace and the fact that his father was deceased at the time of application. It provided great clues to assist a descendant in pushing further up the family tree.

Here's a little more information about passport application from NARA's website:

> Passport applications may provide important information and clues.

Foreign travel in the nineteenth century was much more frequent than

[FORM FOR NATURALIZED CITIZEN.]

No. 43246   Issued Jan 2. 1875

UNITED STATES OF AMERICA.

one might expect. Overseas travelers included businessmen, the middle class, and naturalized U.S. citizens who returned to their homelands to visit relatives. For example, statistics show that the State Department issued 130,360 passports between 1810 and 1873, more than 369,844 between 1877 and 1909, and more than 1,184,085 between 1912 and 1925. It is unknown how many American citizens traveled abroad with passports issued by state or judicial authorities prior to 1856 or without any passport prior to 1918.

Although 95 percent of mid-19th century passport applicants were men, many women also traveled overseas. If the applicant was to be accompanied by his wife, children, servants, or other females under his protection, their names, ages, and relationship to the applicant were stated on the passport application. One passport was then issued to cover the whole group. Likewise, when children traveled abroad solely with their mother, their names and ages were indicated on the mother's passport application. Passport applications by women in their own names became more frequent in the latter part of the nineteenth century, and by 1923 women constituted over 40 percent of passport applicants.

Note that even though group passports were issued to individuals travel-ing with other family members, important genealogical information was often included for the accompanying family members – name, age and relationship to the passport applicant.

Here are a few more thoughts on passport applications you may wish to keep in mind as you seek applications for your immigrant ancestors:

1. With a few war-time exceptions, passports were not required for American citizens until 1941. There was a seven-month period during the Civil War (August 1861 to March 1862) where passports were required, and again from 1918 through 1921 during World War I.

2. Aliens were not allowed to have passports. There were two periods of exception to this law: from March 1863 to May1866, and again from March 1907 until June 1920. During those periods, individuals who had filed their declaration of intent, but had not yet been naturalized, were able to procure a passport. Few passports were issued to aliens during these time periods, however.

3. Passports were valid for two years, so check across the span of your ancestor's life for applications.

4. If your ancestor was naturalized, information about his/her naturalization will likely be on the passport application.

5. If an individual was naturalized as a result of their father's naturalization while they were a minor, that information will usually be provided on the passport application.

6. Occasionally past errors are noted on passport applications. For example, I have seen passport applications that indicated that the individual's name was misspelled on his naturalization certificate – incredible information to have.

7. As noted earlier, even the earliest passport applications usually included a physical description of the applicant. Photographs have been required since December 21, 1914.

8. Many early passport applications were not much more than handwritten letters with varying amounts of information.

7. FINDING RECORDS

Through the course of this book, I have pointed out various records that can be used to find information about your immigrant ancestors. As I have done so, I have often mentioned that I went to this source (Fold3. com, Ancestry.com, the NARA website, etc.) or that source to find the records that I was illustrating at the time. Rather than make you weed back through those various chapters to find how and where to look for the various records, I decided to pull all that information together in one place – this chapter.

So – read on for source-by-source information on how and where to find those records. Where appropriate, I have also included the URL that will get you to the point I describe. My one caveat is that I have learned through experience that URLs change frequently. If you type in the URL and get a broken link, I have also included how to navigate to that point within the source, so hopefully, between one or the other set of directions, you'll be able to find your way there.

Before getting into source-specific information, let's first cover some of the necessities you need for any of these records. You won't always have every one of them, but the more of them you can use to search for your immigrant ancestors the greater your chances of finding the information you are seeking.

Name. That seems obvious, but it is more complicated than that. If I am looking for one of my McQuillan ancestors, it would be helpful to know a first name to go along with the surname. Also, I cannot afford to get tied into only one spelling of the first and last name. Is it Elizabeth

Be flexible on spelling of names; use wildcards when available.

Meyer, or Elisabeth Maier? If I am too inflexible, I am likely to miss this person in whatever records I am searching for her. Many of the search engines used to comb indices offer the use of wild card characters. So, for example, Eli*abeth M**er would yield results for Elizabeth Meyer as well as for Elisabeth Maier.

Be aware of shortened names and diminutives or nicknames that may have been used. My great grandfather was Edgar Estil Quillen. Yet I have seldom seen him use Edgar on the records he created or that were created for him. Usually he simply wrote Ed Quillen. His wife, Theodora Charity McCollough Quillen always used her nickname – Dolly. And perhaps James Leroy Hansen never went by James or Jim, but by Jimmy. So – be careful not to limit yourself based on a search of only one way the name was spelled or used.

Be open to all the variant spellings possible. Earlier in this book I used the example of my third and fourth great grandfathers, who, living next door to one another, both had their last names spelled incorrectly: Qulline and Quilling. Look for your ancestors under both the name they used after immigration as well as the name used in their native country. Searching for Juan Garcia may yield the results I need when John (or Jon) Garcia won't.

Birth date. When I search for my ancestors, I usually ignore the exact birth date of my ancestor in my search criteria, because using it may cause me to miss him or her. Perhaps a spouse or parent was giving the birth information for an individual in a particular record, and didn't remember correctly. Recall the example I used with the Adam McQuillan family. In two separate documents, Adam gave different birth years for his wife, and neither matched the date that she herself provided. The birthdates of at least one of his sons also varied. Better to leave that off while searching, but keep it to compare with any information you find.

Age. If you know the age your ancestor would have been during the creation of a certain record (passenger list, declaration of intent, etc.), you can use that as one of your search criterion. However, most search engines allow you to say such and such an age, give or take X years (usually 1, 2, 5 or even 10 years). So if you think your ancestor was born around 1850, put 1850 down, but select the option to add or subtract 2 years. If that search yields no results, add 5 years.

Birth place. It's helpful to know your ancestor's birthplace. If you know your immigrant ancestor was born in Scotland, you can probably ignore anyone whose birth place comes up as Morocco. (But be open to that possibility!)

Arrival Date. As we've discussed in earlier chapters, the date of an immigrant's arrival is key to finding records that may provide important genealogical information. Many records ask how long the immigrant has been in the United States: censuses, voter registration records, even death certificates. This information may help narrow your search for other records that provide more specific information.

Port of Entry. Like your immigrant ancestor's date of arrival, knowing the port of entry through which your ancestor entered the country may give you a starting point for locating further information in passenger lists, declarations of intent, etc.

Googling

While Googling (or Yahooing, or Binging, etc.) may seem like more of a shotgun approach, I would encourage you not to dismiss it, especially when your efforts to find a certain record through more targeted searches yield little or no information. A source that NARA lists as only available on microfilm that can be viewed at certain regional NARA locations may have been transcribed by a genealogy society for a town, county or even state. So Googling *New Orleans passenger lists*, for example, may yield results that are otherwise unavailable online. And if it is not online today, it may be tomorrow or next week or next month.

Where to find Passenger Lists

Google is a great genealogical search engine!

NARA. We discussed the many ports of entry through which your immigrant ancestors may have entered the United States. The passenger lists for many of those ports may be online, or they may be on microfilm at NARA (National Archives and Records Administration).

NARA has immigration passenger lists from 1820 through 1982 on microfilm. Their records are arranged by port of arrival. You can go to *www.archives.gov/research/immigration* to learn more about what is available through NARA, but here is a summary:

1. Immigration records are kept by port of entry into the United States.

2. Microfilmed copies of passenger lists up to 1955 are available at the National Archives in Washington DC, and some may be available at regional NARA locations. A link from the NARA site will take you to their microfilm catalog so you can see whether certain passenger list microfilms are available at one of the regional facilities.

If you aren't close enough to a regional NARA facility to visit personally, you can order copies of passenger arrival records by using order form NATF 81, or by ordering online. In addition, the information contained about various passenger lists will let you know whether those records are available online (most are not yet available through NARA) through some other subscription service, such as Ancestry.com and Fold3.com.

From the NARA website, you can search the various ports of entry to see what records they have, and to also see what facilities have copies of the microfilmed records. Many records can be found at any of NARA's fourteen regional facilities, while others are located at only selected facilities.

NARA has a little over 6 million records for immigrants in their *Access to*

Archival Databases (AAD) collection. It is found at *http://aad.archives. gov/aad/*. In the center of the page (under *Browse by Category*), under *Genealogy/Personal History*, click on *Passenger lists*, and you'll be introduced to four collections currently held by NARA. Select a collection, then enter your search criteria. The URL is *http://aad.archives.gov/aad/ series-list.jsp?cat=GP44*.

Castlegarden.org. Castle Garden was the immigration processing, New York port of arrival predecessor to Ellis Island. Castle Garden processed over 11 million immigrants the seventy-two years their doors were open – from 1820 to 1892. You'll find transcriptions of the passenger lists for those who entered the United States through Castle Garden. The website is pretty straight-forward – go to *www.castlegarden.org*, click Search and then enter your criteria. You'll find it at *www.castlegarden.org/searcher.php*.

Ellisisland.org. Ellis Island is the most well-known of the ports of entry for immigrants, and with good reason – over 12 million immigrants were processed through her gates. Like Castle Garden, the website is pretty intuitive. Go to *www.ellisisland.org*, and enter the name of the ancestor whom you are seeking. You'll be taken to a login page, so you'll have to either register or log in (there is no cost). From there, you'll see the results of your request. There is no fee for using Ellisisland.org, although there are some records-related items you can purchase if you wish: pictures of ships, pictures of the pages on which your ancestor's name appears, etc.

Ancestry.com has a collection of passenger lists, in particular those for the New York ports as well as other high-volume ports – Boston, Baltimore, Philadelphia and New Orleans. To search those lists, go to *www. Ancestry.com*. From the main page, click on the *Search* tab, then click on *Immigration & Travel*. On the right-hand side of the page click on *Passenger Lists*; once you're there, begin entering information that will identify your immigrant ancestor. Once you have entered the information, click on *Search* at the bottom of the form and see what information they have. The URL for this search page is *http://search.ancestry.com/ search/category.aspx?cat=40*.

As of this writing, Ancestry.com has a number of rates for varying levels of records access. Rates for their most basic US Records Research are $19.99/month or $99 for six month's access. For access to their World Records collection, the cost is $34.99/month or $149 for a six-month subscription. Their Cadillac plan includes their World Records collection as well as subscriptions to Fold3 and Newspapers.com, and that runs $44.99/month or $199 for a six-month subscription.

Fold3.com used to have a nice collection of passenger lists, but since their acquisition by Ancestry.com, those collections are no longer available at Fold3.com. It's still an awesome website for military records, but just not passenger lists. They do have a nice collection of naturalization papers, however. You get to Fold3 by going to *www.Fold3.com*.

At the time of this writing, there are two levels of service: the first is free, and it provides access to many records. However for full access to their online records, a subscription to Fold3 will run you $7.95 a month, or $79.95 for an annual subscription.

FamilySearch.org is the genealogy website of the LDS Church, also has passenger lists. To find them, go to *www.FamilySearch.org*, select *Search* then select *Catalog*. Under *Search by*, select *Keywords*. In the box that appears, type *New York passenger lists* (or whatever port you think your ancestor may have come through), then click *Search*. That will take you to a listing of FamilySearch's collection of *New York passenger lists*. Choose the collection you wish to search, then complete the search criteria. FamilySearch may have transcriptions of the record, and may possibly have an image of the passenger list you can view online. There is no cost to use FamilySearch.

Google. Again, be sure to Google passenger lists, preferably using the name of the port of entry where you believe your ancestor may have entered the United States.

Where to find Naturalization Records

As you search for naturalization records, remember that there are two primary types of naturalization records – declarations of intent and petitions for citizenship (also called petitions for naturalization). It is good to remember that the first papers (declaration of intent) were often filed in or near the city where the immigrant arrived in the United States, while the second papers (petitions for citizenship) were filed in or near the place where the immigrant settled (which was often many miles away from their original port of entry).

NARA. Once again, NARA is a key location for naturalization records. Prior to 1906, many naturalization records were filed in other than federal courts – municipal, county and state courts. After 1906, the federal courts began processing naturalizations. To discover what collections NARA has, go to *www.archives.gov/research/*. In the *Search* box, type *Naturalizations*, and you'll be taken to the government's naturalizations collection. The URL to get you to this point is *http://search.archives.gov/ query.html?col=1arch&col=social&qt=New+York+naturalizations&charse t=iso-8859-1&qc=1arch+social&image.x=0&image.y=0*.

Select the collection you believe may contain information about your immigrant ancestor and click on it. You'll be taken to an information page for that collection, and you'll learn whether the collection is for rent or sale. The right-hand side of the page will tell you what facilities that particular collection may be viewed at. Note that generally speaking, not all regional NARA facilities have access to all microfilms.

Online Searchable Naturalization Indexes and Records. This is a nifty website that helps you find naturalization records across the nation. You'll find it at www.germanroots.com/naturalization.html. Many naturalization records are held at the town, city, county or state level, and this website provides a state-by-state listing of available online naturalization records. Many of the records are transcriptions of the actual naturalization document. If you find an immigrant ancestor's information on this website, you would likely want to follow up by contacting the entity that has the document and get a copy. Listed on the website are the online naturalization records held by each state, with links to the various sites listed.

Fold3.com. Fold3 has an agreement with NARA to bring many of NARA's records online, and they have a nice naturalization records collection. To get to their collection, go to *www.Fold3.com*, then click on *Browse*. Select *Naturalizations 1700s to mid-1900s*, and click on it. To get to that point, the URL is *www.Fold3.com/browse.php#39*. From there, there are columns from which you can select, depending on what you are looking for. For example, the first column provides two choices: *Indexes and Documents*. If you select Documents, another column appears, listing the various districts for which they have records (New York Eastern, New York Southern, Los Angeles, etc.). Selecting one of them further narrows your search by allowing you to select the country of birth of your ancestor. You may stop at any point by typing the surname or your immigrant ancestor in the Search box in the center of the page. Note that the further you narrow your search parameters, you will get fewer and fewer records to review.

State-by-state listing of online naturalization records: *www.german-roots.com/naturalization. html*

However, if you narrow it too much, you may eliminate your ancestor through a misspelling, incorrect date or place, etc. If you try a very narrow search and you come up empty, back up and throw a wider loop for your immigrant ancestor.

Ancestry.com. Ancestry also has a collection of naturalization records. Go to their main page, and click on *Search*. Click on *Card Catalog*. At the top of the left-hand column, type *Naturalization* in the *Title* box, and you'll be shown the various naturalization collections that Ancestry has. Click on the *Search* tab, then select *Immigration & Travel,* then complete the search section with the criteria you would like to have searched.

Where to find Alien Enemy Registration Records

Alien enemy registration records can be found online by Googling *alien registration records, World War I* or *alien registration records, World War II*. Many states have put their alien registration records online, or at least abstracts and transcriptions thereof.

You can access these forms in any number of ways. They are the property of the federal government and are in the government archives. Go to *www.archives.gov/research/arc/index.html*, and type in the name of your immigrant ancestor, and see if he or she completed a registration form – the forms were four pages long (including a page for fingerprints). In the search box on the National Archives and Records Administration (NARA) site, I just used an ancestor's surname along with the word alien: *McQuillan alien*, and got a number of hits.

Not all records have been digitized, but many have been. If you locate an ancestor who filed a *Registration Affidavit of Alien Enemy* form or a *Registration Affidavit of Alien Female* on the NARA site and they are not available online, you will be able to see which regional National Archives sites have a copy of the microfilm for viewing. In addition, genealogy societies all over the US have found the transcription of these forms to be a great project, and many of the abstracts and transcriptions are finding their way online.

Alien Enemy Registration records = overlooked records offering great potential.

8. A SMALL CASE STUDY

Throughout the course of this book, we have looked at various and sundry records that may yield important information on your immigrant ancestors. Many have centered around immigration and naturalization records of different sorts.

I often receive e-mails from my readers, requesting forms (mentioned in *Secrets of Tracing Your Ancestors*) as well as questions about research and ways to overcome brick walls. I thought I would add one of those e-mails I received while writing this book, as much of my response dealt with some of the very topics we have discussed in previous chapters.

Here's the initial e-mail (I received permission from the author to share this):

> Hello, my name is Jonie and I read your book, *Secrets Of Tracing Your Ancestors*.
>
> I have been trying to find my great grandfather on a passenger list, his name was John Gottlieb Kleinknecht.
>
> He was born in Germany, but I am not sure exactly where at in Germany. He was born 30 October 1838. A sister at the LDS Family History Center found his christening records, and according to them he was born in Oberth (Oberweissach). I am not sure if that is a German state, town or what!?

His father's name was Johannes, his mother's name was Anna Maria, but I am not sure of her last name!

The next info I got was that he filed for application, in the Wuerttemberg, Germany Emigration index, March 1858, District, Backnang. His destination was North America.

I found his application to become a citizen in Mahoning County, Ohio, on 22 June, 1861, but no information on his trip over, no dates, nothing!

He married my great grandmother Hanna Myers 1 January 1863. They were married in Mahoning County, Ohio.

On 9 January 1864, John was a citizen of the United States.

I have looked through some other records and he gives the name of his father as Christian. I am thinking it may have been Johannes Christian Kleinknecht, but on his death records (filled out by one his daughters), she did not know her grandmother's name. That hit me as very strange, that his daughter knew her grandfather's name but not her grandmother's name?

He died 3 November 1914.

So my question is how do I find him coming to North America? I have checked passenger lists from March 1858 to June 1861. I know that I may never find him, which means I can't confirm that the information found by the lady at the LDS Family History Center is in fact my John Gottlieb Kleinknecht. And it stops my research for lost relatives in Germany, which makes me very sad!

If you have any ideas, please let me know, and thank you for reading my email.

Given the topics of this book, and any other genealogy research methods you can think of, how would you answer Jonie's inquiry? Following is my answer. Hopefully it demonstrates some of the things we have been focusing on throughout this book:

Hello Jonie,

Thanks for buying my book (or at least checking it out of the library!), but even bigger thanks for actually reading it!

A couple of thoughts....

First of all — congratulations — you have already found more information on John than most researchers would have found! Good for you. You might try to find his obituary in a local newspaper near where he died — sometimes they shed some additional light on the individual and/or his family.

It does seem a bit odd that his daughter didn't know her grandmother's name, although if her grandmother died years before, she may have only known her as Grandma, or Grandma Kleinknecht. (Actually – she may have known her as *Oma* or *Oma Kleinknecht*. *Oma* is a German term of endearment for a grandmother – sort of like Grammy.)

Oberweissach is not a German state, it is a town. Here's a link to a Wiki article on it: *http://en.wikipedia.org/wiki/Oberwei%C3%9Fbach*. It is in central Germany. You should go visit it!

The LDS genealogy site, *www.FamilySearch.org*, has a lot of information on doing German research. I'd suggest checking that out to see if you can find anything that will help you further your research. Go to the website, and click *Learn*, then type in *Germany*. Or maybe even try *Oberweissach*, but that may be too fine a search.

Also, you say he became a citizen in 1864 (or at least was one as of that date), and also that he made application in 1861. That's curious, since his emigration records from Wuerttemberg were in 1858. Except in very special circumstances, immigrants had to wait five years before applying for citizenship...if he applied for citizenship in 1861, that means John may have come as early as 1856, maybe earlier — and the 1858 emigration information you found was when he returned to fetch his family and bring them back with him. Maybe? (Isn't this fun — like being a detective!) Also, since he became a citizen in 1864, perhaps he served during the Civil War (many Germans did) and got his citizenship that way. If he was a soldier in the US army (if he served, since he was living in Ohio it is probable that he would have fought for the North), he only had to serve one year and be honorably discharged to qualify for citizenship. You might want to check to see if he or his wife filed for a pension. There is usually good genealogy information available in pension applications.

I would try to find him in the 1900 and 1910 censuses — both asked important questions about immigrants. In 1900, the questions asked were:

- If an immigrant, the year of immigration to the United States.
- How long the immigrant has been in the United States.
- Is the person naturalized?

In 1910, here were the questions:

- Year of immigration to the United States
- Whether naturalized or alien

Answers to some of those questions might give you some more clues! I just Googled John and lo and behold – I found your Facebook posting about him. That's a good thing to do, also!

Finally — don't give up. If something isn't available now, it may be later on. New websites and new information come online daily, and maybe the website and info you are looking for isn't yet online.

Those are my thoughts at this moment. If any others come to me, I'll shoot you another e-mail.

Good luck, Jonie! Even though you're a little discouraged at the moment, you have made outstanding progress on this ancestor of yours!

Dan Quillen
"I seek dead people."

As you can see, this reader had already gotten some great information on her great grandfather. She was hoping to confirm that information, and then to take that information further back, continuing her journey along her family tree.

What other thoughts do you have about where this reader can go to find information about her ancestor? Other sources that come to mind for me include:

1. Genealogy societies. It is possible that some Mahoning County, Ohio genealogy society has done research on some of its pioneering citizens.

2. German genealogy societies. I suspect there are several German Genealogy Societies in Ohio. Perhaps they have plowed some of the genealogical ground and found – and published — some of the information about Mr. Kleinknecht.

3. County histories. Perhaps a county history of Mahoning County was written that includes information about Mr. Kleinknecht. These were popular in the latter quarter of the 18th century – 1875 through 1900 – and he might have been a great subject for an article.

4. Newspapers. I mentioned obituaries in my response to Jonie, but there may have been other articles written about Mr. Kleinknecht through the years. Was he an attorney hanging out his shingle, a bookkeeper advertising for new clients? Did he open a retail outlet? Was one of his children married, and he and his wife mentioned in the accompanying article? Did he run for office after his naturalization? If so, a short biographical sketch may have accompanied information about him and his political views.

5. Declaration of intent. Jonie doesn't mention finding a declaration of intent – John's *first papers*. That might shed some additional light on her immigrant ancestor's birth location, perhaps some genealogical information about other family members. As you saw in my exchange with her, there may be an issue of when he actually came to America the first time. I suspect he came at least once prior to his emigration information might indicate in the Hamburg passenger lists.

6. Passport application. It might be worth checking to see if John applied for a passport, to return to Germany for any reason. Perhaps he returned to settle an estate, to vacation or to simply see family members. As we've seen on some of the applications included earlier in this book, perhaps he left a business that needed attending to years after he arrived in America.

And how about you – what other sources can you think of that will assist Jonie in finding information about this important immigrant ancestor? If you think of anything I have overlooked (I am sure there is a lot I have overlooked!), e-mail me at *wdanielquillen@gmail.com*.

9. GLOSSARY OF TERMS

Blog – short for Web Log, an online journal or "log" kept and generally shared with the public, or a close group of friends and family.

Browser – a method for accessing the World Wide Web (www.....)

Bulletin Board – see also Message Board. A place where you can go online to seek and share information; in this context – genealogy information.

Censuses – enumerations of the populaton taken in the years after an immigrant's arrival may contain valuable clues to finding immigration and naturalization papers completed by the immigrant. The census itself is full of genealogical value, but may lead you to other documents that will expand that information exponentially.

Certificates of Arrival – these were short notices containing the immigrant's name, date of departure and arrival, port of departure and entry and the name of the ship on which they traveled. Very little information of genealogical value is to be found on certificates of arrival, but they may lead you to other more helpful documents.

Database – a collection of information that can be searched in many ways – by name, date of birth, birth place, etc.

Declaration of Intent — these were papers completed to indicate the immigrant's intention to become a US citizen. They were often completed immediately upon arrival in the US, but were sometimes completed later. These are often called *first papers*. These papers usually have a great deal of genealogical information in them.

E-mail – Electronic Mail. A communication medium very popular with genealogists, who send messages from their computer to another's computer. Delivery is generally more or less instantaneous.

Emigration records – those records created when an individual left a country to take up residence someplace else. Sometimes they provide significant information, sometimes they do not. Don't overlook them when searching for your immigrant ancestors.

Family Group Sheet – a collection of genealogical information about an individual, usually grouped with his or her family (parents, spouse, children).

Final papers — these papers were completed by the immigrant as part of his or her formal request to become a US citizen. Generally speaking, these could not be completed until an immigrant had been in the US at least five years. Also called *second papers*, as well as *Petition for Naturalization* or *Petition for Citizenship*. These papers usually have a great deal of genealogical information in them.

GEDCOM – acronym for **GE**nealogical **D**ata **COM**munication. The standard protocol and format for transferring genealogy information electronically between software packages.

Immigration records – those records created when an individual came to a new country with the intent to live there. Examples of immigration records include Declaration of Intent, Petition for Naturalization, Petition for Citizenship, Oath of Allegiance, etc.

LDS – common acronym for the Latter-day Saints, more formally known as The Church of Jesus Christ of Latter-day Saints, more informally known as the Mormon Church.

National Archives and Records Administration (NARA) – this is the federal organization charged with preserving the nation's important historical documents. Many records of significant genealogical value can be found here. This is the source of many of the genealogy records available (or not!) to genealogists.

Naturalization records – these are records completed by immigrants in search of United States citizenship. They often contain valuable genealogical information about the immigrant as well as his or her family.

Oath of Allegiance – this is the document the immigrant signs as s/he becomes a US citizen, renouncing his allegiance to any other foreign power, dignitary, king, etc. Very little information of a genealogical value is contained in Oaths of Allegiance, but there may be some clues that will lead you to other sources of information.

Pedigree Chart – a chart that linearly shows the ancestry of an individual, from himself or herself back from one generation to the next.

Petition for Citizenship – these papers were completed by the immigrant as part of his or her formal request to become a US citizen. Generally speaking, these could not be completed until an immigrant had been in the US at least five years. Also called *second papers* or *final papers*, as well as *Petition for Naturalization*. These papers usually have a great deal of genealogical information in them.

Petition for Naturalization – these papers were completed by the immigrant as part of his or her formal request to become a US citizen. Generally speaking, these could not be completed until an immigrant had been in the US at least five years. Also called *second papers* or *final papers*, as well as *Petition for Citizenship*. These papers usually have a great deal of genealogical information in them.

Passenger lists – these are the rosters of all who traveled on ships to the United States. They are sometimes called *ship manifests*. These records, especially in later immigration years, may contain a great deal of information of genealogical value.

Primary Source – genealogy records created at the time of the event. A birth certificate would be considered a primary source for birth date and birth place.

Search Engine – a program used to search the World Wide Web for information and data.

Second papers — these papers were completed by the immigrant as part of his or her formal request to become a US citizen. Generally speaking, these could not be completed until an immigrant had been in the US at least five years. Also called *final papers*, as well as *Petition for Naturalization* or *Petition for Citizenship*. These papers usually have a great deal of genealogical information in them.

Secondary Source – genealogy records where information is provided much later than the event. A tombstone or death certificate would be considered a primary source for death information, but a secondary source for birth information, since it is likely that the birth information was provided many years after the person's birth occurred.

Ship manifests – these are the rosters of all who traveled on ships to the United States. They are sometimes called *ship passenger lists*, or *passenger lists*. These records, especially in later immigration years, may contain a great deal of information of genealogical value.

URL – also called universal resource locator, or uniform resource locator. This is the address of a website. Most often it will start with *http:// www.* _____, although sometimes the www is not included in the address.

Vital Records – this is the term used to identify documents that contain information about an individual's birth, marriage or death.

INDEX

GENEALOGICAL NOTES

GENEALOGICAL NOTES

GENEALOGICAL NOTES

GENEALOGICAL NOTES

SALOON, CABIN, AND STEERAGE ALIENS MUST BE COMPLETELY MANIFESTED.

LIST OR MANIFEST OF ALIEN PASSENGERS FOR THE UNITED

Required by the regulations of the Secretary of Commerce and Labor of the United States, under Act of Congress approved February 20, 1907, to be delivered

S.S. *President Grant*   sailing from *Hamburg*   *October 31st* 1909

THE UNITED STATES OF AMERICA

No. 3047487

TO BE GIVEN TO THE PERSON NATURALIZED.

CERTIFICATE OF NATURALIZATION

Petition, Volume 28 Number 7158,

Description of holder: Age, 24 years; height, 5 feet, 0 inches; color, WHITE; complexion, dark; color of eyes, brown; color of hair, black; visible distinguishing marks, none

Name, age, and place of residence of wife

(NOTE: AFTER SEPTEMBER 22, 1922, HUSBAND'S NATURALIZATION DOES NOT MAKE WIFE A CITIZEN.)

Names, ages and places of residence of minor children

ORIGINAL

STATE OF NEW YORK
COUNTY OF ONEIDA } SS:

Victor Serrao (Signature of Holder)

Be it remembered, that Victor Serrao then residing at number 614 Elizabeth Street, city of Utica, State of NEW YORK, who previous to his naturalization was a subject of Italy having applied to be admitted a citizen of the United States of America pursuant to law, and at a SPECIAL term of the court of ONEIDA COUNTY held at UTICA N.Y. on the day of JUN in the year of our Lord nineteen hundred and 29, the court having found that the petitioner intends to reside permanently in the United States and that he had in all respects complied with the Naturalization Laws of the United States, and that he was entitled to be so admitted, it was thereupon ordered by the said court that he be admitted as a citizen of the United States of America.

[SEAL]

In testimony whereof the seal of said court is hereunto affixed on the day of JUN in the year of our Lord nineteen hundred and 29, and of our Independence the one hundred and 53

F. J. Wagner Clerk
Wm W. McDermott Deputy
(Official character of attestor)

DEPARTMENT OF LABOR

Certified Copy of an Entry of Birth,

Pursuant to the Births and Deaths Registration Acts, 1836 to 1874.

Superintendent Registrar's District ... Petersburg

Birth in the Sub-District of ... Kensington ... in the County of ... Mddx.

1909

No.	When and Where Born	Name, if any	Sex	Name and Surname of Father	Name and Maiden Surname of Mother	Rank or Profession of Father	Signature, Description, and Residence of Informant	When Registered	Signature of Registrar	Baptismal Name if added after Registration of Birth
	Fifteenth November 1908 Stratford Road W.8	Jack Matthew	Boy	Frances Tom Brooke	Florence Mary Brooke formerly Bryant	Mechanical Engineer	H.T. Brooke Father ...... Kensington 31 Stratford Road	1909 Registrar.	Haylorth Registrar.	

I, Frederic Elizabeth Haylorth, Registrar of Births and Deaths for the Sub-District of Kensington ...... in the County of Mddx., Do hereby Certify that this is a True Copy of the Entry No. 265 in the Register Book of Births for the said Sub-District, and that such Register Book is now legally in my custody.

Witness my Hand this Fifteenth day of February A.D. 1909.

The Statutory Fees payable for an ordinary certified copy of an entry in a Register of Births, Deaths, or Marriages, if taken at the time of registration, are 1s. (including the fee for the search) or, if taken afterwards, an additional fee of 1s. is chargeable for a search extending over a period of not more than one year, and 6d. additional for every additional year.

Haylorth Registrar.

Published by Arthur Guild, Uppercott, Oxford.

Revised by the Registrar-General.

COLD SPRING PRESS GENEALOGY BOOKS

Secrets of Tracing Your Ancestors, 7th Edition, $14.95
The Troubleshooter's Guide to Do-It-Yourself Genealogy, 3rd Edition,
$14.95

Quillen's Essentials of Genealogy series offers the following books:
• *Mastering Online Genealogy*, 3rd Edition, $12.95
• *Mastering Immigration & Naturalization Records*, 3rd Edition, $12.95
• *Mastering Census & Military Records*, 3rd Edition, $12.95
• *Tracing Your European Roots*, 2nd Edition, $11.95
• *Tracing Your Irish & British Roots*, 2nd Edition, $9.95
• *Mastering Family, Library, & Church Records*, 2nd Edition, $12.95

All our books available in major bookstores, online booksellers, or
through our website at *www.essentialgenealogy.com*.